ROOM FOR ALL OF US

ALSO BY ADRIENNE CLARKSON

Heart Matters

Norman Bethune

ADRIENNE CLARKSON

ROOM FOR ALL OF US

SURPRISING STORIES OF LOSS AND TRANSFORMATION

ALLEN LANE
CANADA

ALLEN LANE CANADA

Published by the Penguin Group

Penguin Group (Canada), 90 Eglinton Avenue East, Suite 700, Toronto, Ontario, Canada M4P 2Y3
(a division of Pearson Canada Inc.)

Penguin Group (USA) Inc., 375 Hudson Street, New York, New York 10014, U.S.A.
Penguin Books Ltd, 80 Strand, London WC2R 0RL, England
Penguin Ireland, 25 St Stephen's Green, Dublin 2, Ireland (a division of Penguin Books Ltd)
Penguin Group (Australia), 250 Camberwell Road, Camberwell, Victoria 3124, Australia
(a division of Pearson Australia Group Pty Ltd)
Penguin Books India Pvt Ltd, 11 Community Centre, Panchsheel Park, New Delhi – 110 017, India
Penguin Group (NZ), 67 Apollo Drive, Rosedale, Auckland 0632, New Zealand
(a division of Pearson New Zealand Ltd)
Penguin Books (South Africa) (Pty) Ltd, 24 Sturdee Avenue, Rosebank, Johannesburg 2196, South Africa

Penguin Books Ltd, Registered Offices: 80 Strand, London WC2R 0RL, England

First published 2011

1 2 3 4 5 6 7 8 9 10 (RRD)

Copyright © Adrienne Clarkson, 2011

Author representation: Westwood Creative Artists
94 Harbord Street, Toronto, Ontario M5S 1G6

Excerpts from poetry by Pablo Neruda and Claudio Duran used with permission.

Manufactured in the U.S.A.

LIBRARY AND ARCHIVES CANADA CATALOGUING IN PUBLICATION

Clarkson, Adrienne, 1939–
Room for all of us : surprising stories of loss and transformation / Adrienne Clarkson.

Includes bibliographical references and index.
ISBN 978-0-670-06547-9

1. Clarkson, Adrienne, 1939–. 2. Immigrants—Canada—Biography.
3. Canada—Emigration and immigration.
4. Cultural pluralism—Canada. I. Title.

FC104.C53 2011   920.071   C2011-905471-X

Visit the Penguin Group (Canada) website at **www.penguin.ca**

Special and corporate bulk purchase rates available; please see
www.penguin.ca/corporatesales or call 1-800-810-3104, ext. 2477 or 2474

FOR
TALIA, MYLO, THEO, AND KAI,
who will inherit the Canada
that the people in this book are creating

CONTENTS

OUT OF CATACLYSM
AND CATASTROPHE

This book is about people like me. When I published *Heart Matters*, in 2006, many people told me they thought it was a great story and that it showed how unusual my path had been in Canada. Even close friends went out of their way to say that they thought my story was different from anything anyone else had experienced in Canada. My immediate reaction was to disagree. All of my life, I've met people who have lived trajectories not exactly like mine but in their own way, just as remarkable. Like me, the people in this book came out of cataclysm and catastrophe not of their own making and found themselves almost thrown into Canada. And what did Canada do? Canada took us in, and our real lives began. I told my story because I wanted people to identify with it and realize that they, too, had come a long way. I wanted to show that the goals they may never have thought possible, proved attainable because they were Canadian.

The people I write about were almost surprised by the way their lives turned out. They had worked hard to succeed and they are a very accomplished group, but what happened to them could only have happened because of their being uprooted and forcibly transplanted to another place. That this place was Canada was very fortuitous. People in every society—whether it is France, which I know well, or Britain, or the United States—can succeed. But there is something particular about Canada, with its atmosphere of benevolent neglect, of letting people alone, that makes it possible for those who arrive with nothing to sense that they can belong and be part of something they can help to construct.

What follows is a simple account of immigrant experiences at the beginning of the twenty-first century, of people who would have died or suffered terribly, and certainly never would have come to the true fullness of their development, had they not been taken in by Canada. These people are immigrants like me. Some of them are refugees like me. All of them depended very much on the kindness of strangers to be taken in and allowed to make their way.

These are stories not just of survival, but of people who had very little choice and had to make the best of what was offered. Whether this meant being picked up in an airplane in Hong Kong and landing in Edmonton in the middle of winter, or being flown from Santiago to Vancouver after a military coup, or fetching up in Montreal as a deserter from the U.S. Army—all of them, like me, were driven here by forces that were out of their control.

Heart Matters was my story—the story of how our family came to Canada with one suitcase each, having been chosen almost at random to board a ship that was part of the Red Cross exchange of civilians on the two sides of the Pacific War. We came to Ottawa and made our way thanks to my father getting a job in the Canadian government. But we really made our way thanks to the people we met by chance and thanks to my parents' enormous strength of character—my father's humour, resilience, and intelligence, and my mother's sensitivity, perfectionism, and struggle against depression. With that guidance and their terrific alertness to all of their surroundings, they sacrificed and saved so that my brother and I could go to university—in his case McGill, to become a doctor, and in mine, Trinity College at the University of Toronto, which led to a career that began in television. Canada did not set up any insurmountable barriers for me. I went to a very good high school, Lisgar Collegiate, in Ottawa, and at Trinity I was able to make friends and penetrate (I think that is the right word) the heart of Canadian life, which I have inhabited ever since. The close friends I made then, at the age of eighteen, have remained part of me through all of the changes in my life.

I don't believe I ever thought I wouldn't be able to do any of this. Canada was, after all, an easy country to live in and to do well in. At first, as a child, that meant excelling at exams and getting scholarships, and later it meant being good on television and the other things that came along to challenge me. I know I wouldn't have had the same kind of life had there been no war and had we remained in Hong Kong, but for many years I didn't think to ask my father what he thought would have become of us had we been able to stay. For us, our adaptation to Canada was so important and overpowering that I wasn't even able to frame the question until about twenty years ago. When I finally did ask him, after we had eaten a quiet dinner together, he answered, "Well, if we'd stayed in Hong Kong, you would have been very clever, and I would have continued to do well in business, and so we probably would have sent you to the States to university—Radcliffe or Vassar or Wellesley." I thought about that for a while. I knew that if I had gone to one of those schools, I would have still done very well academically, but I wouldn't have ended up as Governor-General of Canada! I might just have ended up marrying somebody rich, moving back to Hong Kong, and leading a comfortable life, perhaps immigrating to Canada in my thirties.

None of the people in this book lead lives that resemble what they would have been had they stayed in Germany, Tanzania, Ho Chi Minh City, or Belgrade. The context would have been so different that even the ones who are artists, who might still have produced their art, would not have done it in the same way. Canada gives us a wider berth and a lodging that attaches us into something larger than simply our race or our religion or even our language. I'm convinced it has to do with the geography, the space, that we inhabit and the sense that there is room for all of us.

The empathy I feel with the people in this book reflects, I think, the great bond among all Canadians. With the notable exception of the Aboriginal peoples, we are all immigrants to this country. Our history of immigration has been chequered. At the turn of the twentieth century, we opened our gates and tried to include and welcome people—particularly in the West, where we took in more than a hundred thousand immigrants a year, culminating in the astonishing number of four hundred thousand in 1913. After the Second World War, we did the same, and since the 1980s we have been increasing our population by one percent a year with immigrants from all countries of the world. But these were also years when we passed legislation to restrict immigration, such as discouraging Chinese people from entering Canada at the beginning of the twentieth century by inflicting the notorious Head Tax, the attempt to disinherit the Doukhobors from the land that they had worked and made fruitful for ten years, and our shameful refusal to take in Jews who we knew were being persecuted in the 1930s. But we have been able to change, and it is that ability that distinguishes Canada from many other countries in the world. Once we decided that we were going to be inclusive, we did it without reservation.

Today, in any citizenship ceremony in Canada (and we have 2,900 of them a year), if there are forty-nine new citizens taking the oath, they will come, on average, from twenty-five different countries in the world. This astounding feat is not matched by any other country in the world. Eighty percent of the people who come to Canada take up citizenship. This is the highest rate in the world; the rate is only sixty percent in the United States and seventy-five percent in Australia. People take up citizenship here because they know, after having lived here for three to five years, that we want them to be citizens. We don't declare love to them, because that is not what Canadians do, but they see that they will be at ease here, able to live their lives relatively free of rejection and stereotypes.

When I represented Ontario in France as Agent General in the mid-1980s, I talked to a lot of French politicians about the benefits of our country. The leader of one of the centrist parties in France, the UDF, once said to me indignantly, "Of course, you can afford to take any amount of immigrants. Canada is already a mongrelized country!" I think he's right, and I don't take it as an insult; we should not be ashamed of this. We have drawn strength from all the different people who have come here, even though our bureaucratic policies have shifted back and forth, from exclusionary to inclusive.

We should be mindful and proud of what the most important figures in our democratic past have said to us about immigration. In 1840, Louis-Hippolyte LaFontaine, who would later become the first democratically chosen Canadian prime minister, said in his Address to the Electors of Terrebonne:

> Canada is the land of our ancestors; it is our country as it
> must be the adopted country of the various populations
> which come from diverse portions of the globe, to make their
> way into its vast forests as the future resting place of their
> families and their hopes. Like us, their paramount desire
> must be the happiness and prosperity of Canada, as the
> heritage which they should endeavour to transmit to their
> descendants in this young and hospitable country. Above all,
> their children must be like ourselves, CANADIANS.

In that address 171 years ago are all the principles that Canadians live by in an immigrant society today. Look at the key phrases in it: "Adopted country," "diverse portions of the globe," "the future resting place," "their paramount desire must be the happiness and prosperity of Canada," "this young and hospitable country." Everything we cherish as a country is in that paragraph. It should be our guide as we move further into the twenty-first century, and we should acknowledge that a logical evolution has taken place because of our fundamental belief in what was first enunciated by Louis LaFontaine.

The British Canadians, many of whom were often among the earlier immigrants, were often wary of change that they feared would pull this country away from what they saw as its roots. We should not blame them for hanging on so strongly to their British heritage. It was a colonial mentality that led them to do so: the many benefits of our British heritage, such as common law, parliamentary democracy, and the rights of the individual, are ideas and practices that have helped create a solid infrastructure for our country. That framework has been tried and works with our constitution, one of the oldest and most democratic in the world; it can support the hundreds of different backgrounds that now make up Canada.

People of the world come here and fit into our geography and our heritage of governmental and social structures, but we should never think that they come with nothing. The people you are going to meet in these pages may have emerged from chaos, but they all benefited from a strong family structure and, in most cases, a vibrant extended family structure. Family blended into community in a way that strengthened individuals and made them capable of accomplishing more than they could have on their own.

When Canadians share their stories, it helps us realize that Canada is a place of individual narratives. In this regard, we are unlike countries that have maintained a monolithic status, where everyone is, or pretends to be, one thing: English, French, German. What we are developing in Canada, to the highest degree, is what the Aga Khan in his recent LaFontaine-Baldwin lecture so perceptively called the cosmopolitan ethic. We understand more and more that all immigrants to Canada have their own stories, not only from their countries, but from their villages and from their families. Immigrants bring to Canada a complexity that adds texture and richness to the total fabric of our society. As I sit on a bus or subway and look at the faces around me, I often think that each person has a story worth telling and that we should all hear. I'm telling a few of them here because they represent what the Aga Khan describes so well.

The world can be viewed from a narrow national or racial perspective, but it can also be understood as an independent whole in which each of us has a part to play. Because so many people who become Canadian citizens have memories and roots elsewhere, they can make comparisons, make judgments, help all of us to make choices. If you are brought up in one single culture with one pervasive point of view, it can be stifling. In the world of cyberspace and instant communication, we are the best-placed people in the world to be able to communicate with each other. Because we have been diverse from the very beginning, a mix of Aboriginals, French, English, indigenous spiritualism, Protestant, and Catholic, we have been able to see ourselves as a combination of separate groups and to know what those differences were. And yet behind all of that, we in Canada have been behaving as if we really believed what Aristotle pointed out thousands of years ago: that the human race is a whole. I have come to believe this more and more as I have had occasion to be part of different extraordinary events. When I was Governor-General, giving out the Bravery Awards (which I will talk about later in the book) changed my view of what makes people do extraordinary things.

Our attachment to the wilderness is part of the legacy given to us by the indigenous peoples who guided the first French explorers and then the Hudson Bay Scots into the interior of this enormous continent through the rivers that were its arteries. This entry into the heart of the continent with the graceful welcome of the Aboriginals has, I believe, left an indelible imprint on the way we help others penetrate and become a part of a country in which nature is stronger than any one of us or any group of us. Of course, it's true that nature is stronger than all human beings everywhere, but in Canada, because of the climate and the limits on where human beings can safely live, we feel it even more acutely and it is of even greater importance.

As a result of being Governor-General for six years, I saw a need in Canada to understand why we've become the most successfully diverse country in the world. I'm thinking constantly about what it means to be a citizen of this country. I know for certain that citizenship is not about territory. Yes, of course, our territory happens to be the second largest in the world, but defending its borders is not foremost in mind when we think of what citizenship requires of us. (We are fortunate in this, because we have only one border that we share with another country.) Instead, our notion of citizenship is based on a communal set of values and responsibilities.

Before the First World War, there were no such things as passports. In an interview I did with the historian Arnold Toynbee thirty-two years ago, he recalled that when he went to Greece in 1911 he had a beautiful piece of parchment with a red seal on it from somebody in the British Cabinet who indicated that young Mr. Toynbee was known to him and was of good character and to please let him into any country he wished to enter. That was the way it was then. With borders being drawn, citizenship came to be a label that could be used for exclusion. We are very fortunate that in Canada we are now able to make our citizenship stand for inclusion.

The people you'll meet in this book are distinct in the sense that they have reflected on who they are and what they would have become had they not come to Canada. They acknowledge, either tacitly or vocally, what they have lost, and they know and feel confident about what they have gained. In every case, what they have become in Canada is more than they could ever have achieved in their former lives.

Often their future was determined by the direction their parents wanted them to take and the sacrifices that were made for them; they acknowledge that legacy. I share that appreciation with them. My parents gave me the will and the determination and the confidence to face a new world. They could not possibly have known that Canada would be as negotiable and as welcoming as it turned out to be. With the Vietnamese boat people the Trans, the Mohameds from East Africa, the Sitsabaiesans from Sri Lanka, I share that amazement in the confidence and optimism of my parents. I honestly do not know if I possess that kind of strength.

When I was little, I would often talk to my parents about our coming to Canada and what the voyage had been like. (One of my earliest memories is of seeing a whale on that trip across the Atlantic between South Africa and Brazil.) We arrived in a place that was completely unknown to us, just one small family with a lot of past, a little luggage, and a questionable future. My mother and father are like all the parents I talk about in this book: the mother who sold underwear in occupied Belgium, the father who worked in a box factory in Calgary, the mother who was a maid in hotels, and the father who lost money investing in a motel. I can identify with all of that and want to emphasize that we share this pattern: one generation sets its mind to make sure that the next one can do better. Jung says that the most powerful dynamics in the family are the unrealized dreams of the parents. If this was apparent to Jung when he was dealing with middle-class Swiss people, how much more true is it of immigrant families who have lost everything but survived with their hearts and imaginations intact.

The people in these portraits range in age from twenty-nine to seventy-six, and so I believe that as immigrants they came to two very different Canadas. I came to Canada in the 1940s, as did Fred Bild, to a country that had known terrible poverty during the Depression, then suffered through a world war, before things improved economically for all its people in the 1950s. The Canada I grew up in was much poorer than today, but we were all in the same boat. My family didn't have a car until I was twelve, but that was true of so many of the other kids at school that I didn't notice we didn't have one. The general lack of affluence was a shared way of life. Clothes were either made at home by my mother on her sewing machine or bought during two shopping expeditions a year, one for winter and one for summer—two pairs of shoes, two sweater sets, three skirts, and an overcoat for school. It didn't seem as if we were sacrificing anything, and perhaps that made it easier for us to be immigrants. Most of today's immigrants see an enormous gap between the standard of living where they came from and the material well-being that many of us take for granted in this country and, more disturbingly, feel we are entitled to.

The people in this book have all had to struggle, and all became successful. But I didn't pick them because they were successes; they intrigue me. They represent the variety of world events that propel immigrants here and the kind of choices that face us. And I wanted to tell their stories because of the dignity and imagination and, yes, the courage with which they faced their crises and made their choices. That is the immigrant story: dignity, imagination, and courage before overwhelming events and limited choices. The one fascinating anomaly are the Blairs, an anglophone family with roots two hundred years deep in Quebec, who decided very consciously to become bicultural and bilingual and who feel that Quebec belongs to them as much as to any "pure laine" Quebecer. They did not want to be excluded, so they did everything possible to be included. They faced what to them was the possible disaster of Quebec separating from Canada and made a choice.

The idea of Canada as refuge is an undercurrent in all these stories. People like my family came to this country because they had nothing and, in many cases, no other choice. Even those young

American men seeking to escape service in the Vietnam War felt that they could risk losing their country forever in order to follow their conscience, that what they would be doing in Vietnam would not be right and they had little choice but to leave. This consciousness of knowing that we all start from nothing is the basis of our egalitarianism. We don't begin with a lofty concept. It is in discovering that we can make our place here and not be blocked that helps us immigrants know we are on the same footing as our fellow Canadians. I believe that that conscious egalitarianism is one of the reasons why citizenship has always been encouraged for our immigrants. Our government has usually been wise enough to want our immigrants to become citizens and to have a stake in the country. It began 230 years ago, when our colonial administration gave land to the tens of thousands of refugee Loyalists. This was still going on through the nineteenth century and into the twentieth century with the land given to settlers to make that stake material and eventually prosperous. But this egalitarian idea is also somehow more abstract in its concept of freedom and the ability to learn and to change ourselves without resorting to civil conflict. As a country, we have largely escaped internecine and civil war. In 170-odd years of history since we became a country, eighty people have been killed in civil strife. And of that number, most were killed in one day in the 1880s, during the conflict of Louis Riel's North-West Rebellion.

I feel that Canadians' reluctance to kill each other is a critical subtext in the understanding of our society and values. We are warriors when we need to be, and have proved that in the First and Second World Wars and in the Korean War. And we are very good peacekeepers. But we have never been very good at killing each other. The presence in Canada of French and English, Protestant and Catholic, which in Europe was enough to create bloodbaths, does not seem to have incited us to physical violence. Instead, we have given equal rights to both language groups and religions, and we fight our battles with words and referenda.

This kind of complexity has made it possible for us to become the kind of country we are—open, tolerant, and basically trusting. All of these positive values require effort to maintain. They do not come altogether naturally, but we have, in our understated way, preserved them, and intrinsically we trust them. We have also developed the ability of recognition. In a society where we are all so different from each other, people want to be recognized for what they are, not for what other people see them to be. This is crucial to an individual's, as well as a nation's, sense of identity. As you read these stories, you will see how some of these people were perceived by others and how they dealt with that positive or negative reception. It is crucial that we have this recognition between individuals and also as a nation. Without it, equality becomes mere uniformity.

The philosopher Charles Taylor says, "A prolonged refusal of recognition between groups in a society can erode the common understanding of equal participation on which a functioning liberal democracy crucially depends." A democratic society needs a sense of common citizenship that is based on the recognition of the other. It's important to understand that the other exists, and that the other is not you but outside you and must be part of the society that belongs to both of you.

The Koran tells us that God could have created people with no differences between them but chose not to. "Had God pleased, He could have made of you one community but it is His wish to *test* [italics mine] you by that which He has bestowed upon you" (Koran 5:4). Our differences are not to be feared but welcomed as opening up new avenues of consciousness. We must not deny differences either, or we will be fooling ourselves. And above all, we should not search to erase differences; they challenge us to learn about ourselves through contact with others who are not like us.

People in France, Great Britain, and the United States, well-informed people who were interested in politics and who sometimes held real power, have frequently asked me, "When will it all be resolved in Canada, about Quebec? When will it all be over?" And I always reply, "It is not going to be over. We keep it going, up and down, back and forth, because we really like it that way." I know this is not a satisfying answer to those who are used to revolutions or radical movements solving their political problems. But Canadians have absorbed complexity—two languages, two religions, for starters—to such an extent that living with ambiguity, vexation, and some measure of discomfort is acceptable, and even desirable, to us. There will always be a profound longing in Quebec to be acknowledged by the rest of the world, and the rest of Canada, as an independent and separate entity. It is a constant expression of an inchoate, passionate sense of being. I do not believe it will ever "be over," either as a feeling or as a political position. We who are not Quebecers have to understand this, even as we are alternately annoyed, upset, and exasperated by it. I look on it as basically a family situation in which the various members of that family accept that they each have their own particular qualities. One of them might be the one who always brings up an awkward question at dinner, or the one who always prefers to leave family get-togethers early, or the one who always borrows the car. We are like a family, and our irritations and unhappiness with each other are like those of a family. That is the only way I think it makes sense for Canadians: to look at the totality of Canada with Quebec as part of it. I also believe that our ability to live with unresolved questions makes us conscious that not everybody is alike. I think this is valuable because it adds another layer to our complexity. We may feel irritated by the fact that not everything runs smoothly in our federation, but that makes us more sensitive to what other people are saying and forces us to pay attention.

This ability to understand that society is not just a multiplication of you but includes many who are not like you is vital to a healthy society. This is what we are given a chance to do in Canada, because we see so many people who are not like ourselves, who do not come from the same background. We must search for our common humanity, for the decency, the understanding, and the generosity that must come before making judgments.

We have to understand that this Canadian condition can help us to enlarge our imaginations. Northrop Frye said, "We participate in society by means of our imagination or the quality of our social vision. Our vision of what our society is, what it could be, and what it should be, are all structures of metaphor, because the metaphor is the unit of all imagination. Logical thinking in this field seldom does more than rationalize these metaphorical visions." So we participate. And we see that by having other people participate, even though they're not like us, they have made us a better country.

These are stories of people who have come out of situations in which they were marginalized and sometimes subjected to prejudice and bigotry. Our job in Canada is to try to make sure that nobody, no matter where they are from, is ever the object of any of this. Not only do we want them to pursue their own lives and make their own choices, but we want them to be able to take their place within our society, to learn our values as they have evolved, and most important of all, to add their contribution to society as it changes. And this too is important: that their contribution may make a change that we would never have thought of ourselves and initially might even feel uncomfortable with. We must understand that there are going to be differences and that we have to listen to each other and find out how we can work together to make sure that as long as we are within our democratic heritage we can let them be as they will let us be. Canada is at its best when it offers benevolent neglect so that people find themselves, sometimes stumbling but without obstacles put in their way.

Everybody wants to be included. That is the most important thing for anyone in this country. I do not believe it when people say that certain ethnic or religious groups don't want to be included, that they prefer to live separately. The only reason they could possibly have for not wanting to be included is that they feel so totally excluded that they can't think of how to make the effort to be included. That notion of inclusion is part of our Aboriginal heritage, and it is the Aboriginal people who were able to include us. Chief John Kelly said thirty years ago, "As the years go by, the circle of the Ojibwa gets bigger and bigger. Canadians of all colours and religions are entering that circle. You might feel that you have roots somewhere else, but in reality, you are right here with us."

In 1905, Sir Wilfrid Laurier, the country's first French-Canadian prime minister, gave a speech on the occasion of Alberta and Saskatchewan entering Confederation. At this time, the prairie provinces were filling up with a different type of immigrant: people from Eastern Europe, and also religious minorities like the Doukhobors, the Mennonites, the Hutterites—as diverse a group as the Britishcentric bureaucracy could ever have imagined. Laurier welcomed them with these words:

Those who come at the eleventh hour will receive as fair treatment as those who have been here a long time ... We do not anticipate, and we do not want, that any individuals should forget the land of their origin or their ancestors. Let them look to the past, but let them also look to the future: let them look to the land of their ancestors, but let them also look to the land of their children. Let them become Canadians.

It is this credo that we have been living during most of my lifetime, and it is what I believe we must continue to do. The people in this book have done what Laurier knew they could do— they have become Canadians.

A PRESENT FROM
IDI AMIN

Canadians remember when the dictator Idi Amin expelled thousands of Asians from Uganda in 1972. We, together with Great Britain and several other countries, tried to help. The Asians had only ninety days to organize themselves and were permitted to leave with a maximum of fifty dollars per family and 480 pounds of personal effects. They were citizens of Uganda, but it didn't matter. They were told to leave, and they did so under the protection of the United Nations. Many found refuge in Canada. Some went to transit refugee camps in Europe. About six thousand people ended up in Canada. Many of these Ugandan Asians were Ismailis, a Shiite minority within Islam. The effect of the drastic expulsion reverberated in Ismaili communities in nearby Tanzania, where they, too, began to make preparations to leave.

The Ismailis are a people who have known persecution and diaspora. They belong to a branch of Islam that believes the prophet Muhammad chose his son-in-law Ali, the husband of his daughter Fatima, as his successor and first imam. In the tenth century, the Ismailis established the Fatimid Empire, which had its capital in Cairo and from which the Ismaili imams ruled across the Mediterranean all the way to present-day Pakistan. The Ismailis were able to sustain their community and belief system, and when there was a vigorous revival of Ismaili life in Persia in the early sixteenth century, they came to occupy a place in the Persian hierarchy. In 1817, the forty-sixth imam, Hasan Ali Shah, was granted the title Aga Khan, and it has continued to be passed down to his successors.

During the period of the British Empire, Ismailis spread out from India, where they were concentrated in Gujarat and Bombay, to seek a livelihood in other British colonies. The establishment of Ismailis in East Africa is a direct result of colonialism linking the Gujarat ports on the Arabian Sea to Zanzibar, the East African coast, the Arab countries, Egypt, and eventually Mediterranean Europe. Like all cultures of diaspora, the Chinese or the Jews, for example, the Ismailis formed their own communities and cultural groups. They were also willing to work hard to make a living whenever the opportunity presented itself, and in some cases they made fortunes. Certainly, by the time Idi Amin took power, they felt at home in Uganda. In Tanzania and Kenya as well, they felt that they belonged. They were part of a middle class involved in business and in the government bureaucracy.

Given the extremity of the situation in 1972, the Ismaili spiritual leader and forty-ninth imam, the Aga Khan, intervened to help the Ugandan Asians. He asked Prime Minister Trudeau to help, negotiating with him the acceptance of ten thousand Ismaili refugees. The friendship and trust between the Aga Khan and Trudeau was reflected in the way Ismailis, an unfamiliar group to most Canadians, were received into Canada. At the time, only a few members of the Ismaili community already lived in Canada.

The friendship between Trudeau and the Aga Khan would endure, culminating in the spiritual leader's role as an honorary pallbearer at Trudeau's funeral in 2000. At that funeral, which I attended as Governor-General, we saw an astonishing range of people who had developed relationships with Trudeau and were honorary pallbearers: Fidel Castro, Jimmy Carter, and Leonard Cohen, among others.

Eventually, the Ugandan exiles in Canada were joined by Ismailis arriving from Kenya, Rwanda, Zaire, Madagascar, and Tanzania. Very few remained in East Africa. More Ismailis from South Asia followed, so that today there are more than a hundred thousand Ismailis living in Canada.

For Ismailis, community life mingles the religious and the secular. They meet in buildings they call jamatkhanas, of which there are about seventy-five in small and large communities in Canada. They perform good works that are administered by a national council and various boards that are responsible to the final authority of the Aga Khan. The national council and the boards develop health, education, and economic policies and initiatives, and members of the community serve on them for a given amount of time.

The current Aga Khan has given gender equality high priority. During his fifty-four-year reign, he and his followers have built schools, hospitals, and business, financial, and welfare organizations around the world. He has encouraged his followers to commit themselves fully to the countries in which they have become citizens. In Canada, he is giving his collection of Islamic art to be housed in a new museum in Toronto and has chosen Ottawa to be the seat of the Global Centre for Pluralism, which he has established in partnership with the Canadian government. The Aga

Khan is an honorary Canadian citizen and an honorary companion of the Order of Canada.

This kind of community is the background for two prominent Canadian Ismailis, Naheed Nenshi and Nadir Mohamed.

1
Naheed Nenshi

In October 2010, Calgary witnessed the wonderful and surprising election of Naheed Nenshi as mayor. Still under forty, Naheed was thrust into the spotlight, as was the Ismaili community. Everybody wondered what had precipitated this unexpected event; very few people knew that Naheed had been preparing himself for quite a long time.

John Ralston Saul and I met Naheed Nenshi when he came with a group of some of the brightest twenty-five-year-olds we'd encountered to talk to us at Rideau Hall. They had founded Canada25, a group that wanted to understand and help shape public policy. These young Canadians were working in the arts, in government and consultancy firms, and in universities. They had published a report called *A New Magnetic North: How Canada Can Attract and Retain Young Talent*, which focused on how Canadian cities could become engines of economic development. They held eleven round-table discussions across North America, involving 350 young Canadians.

Naheed was already working at the consulting firm McKinsey & Company, but this Canada25 was part of his community activity. We struck up a friendship. When we went to Calgary on various official visits during my time as Governor-General, we would get in touch with him. So we were not completely surprised when he decided to run for mayor and were thrilled when he was elected. But somehow, with what I would call our Canadian "gradualism" so ingrained in us, we thought that he would first run for city council and a few elections later aim for the mayoralty. Or we thought that he might contest a seat in the provincial legislature. And never did we dream that he would soon capture the imagination of the adventurous Calgarians and become their mayor.

When you look at Naheed, it's hard not to smile. He is positively jolly-looking—curly black hair, dark brown eyes, and a huge smile. His enthusiasm and the speed with which he talks is captivating. It's not so much that this man was born for politics as that politics has a great need of people like him: humane, bright, someone whose eyes actually focus on another person. The word that comes to mind to describe him is "expansive." It feels as though he can take everything in and you are part of his being. This is a rare quality, and it would be a fine thing if more people in public life had it. Perhaps it's not just a quality; perhaps it's actually a gift. Whatever it is, Naheed Nenshi has it.

Naheed will state emphatically that the world needs more Canada. He feels that he experienced an equitable sharing of opportunity, something that would not have been offered in any other country. He knows that no matter how long he might have lived in Japan, he would never be Japanese; that no matter how long he lived in Norway, he would never become Norwegian. But as a first-generation Canadian he has become mayor of a large Canadian city. That openness should not be underrated. Canada, especially Western Canada, offers people the chance to overcome obstacles and move into the future.

Naheed feels fortunate to have come from an ethnic group in which there is a very deeply ingrained ethic of community service and volunteerism. The spiritual drive behind the Ismailis is also the drive that enables them to succeed individually, to be part of the larger community, and to be recognized as leaders.

Naheed says that the Ismailis have always been a minority (Shiite) within a minority (Muslim) within a minority (the Third World), and therefore, they've had to stick together. They have realized that since their diaspora in the thirteenth century, they've become problem-solvers in order to survive. Curiously enough, the volunteer work of the Aga Khan's followers has become what Naheed describes gently as a giant bureaucracy providing all kinds of services. When he was thirty-seven, serving on the National Education Board in Canada for the Aga Khan, he discovered that a lot of young Ismailis who had recently arrived from Central Asia were not succeeding at school. So the board set up a system of nationwide tutorial centres to provide after-school help, and also some mentoring programs. The aim was not only to improve the students' secondary school performance, but to increase rates of admission to post-secondary education. Interestingly enough, the board charged ahead even though there were other non-Ismaili organizations trying to do the same thing. Says Naheed, Ismailis are such self-starters that they don't seek help from other organizations, choosing instead to implement their own programs. He is proud of his community's ability to build something from nothing, but he also warns of the danger of spending time and energy solely in your own community without paying heed to what's happening to the rest of the world. He thinks Ismailis have an obligation to say to others, "We can help you to do this, we can help you bring this kind of success to bear on your own endeavours."

I would characterize the Ismailis, Naheed among them, as amazingly successful overachievers. In 2007, when the Aga Khan was celebrating his golden jubilee as their imam, the Calgarian Ismailis wanted to do something very special. It has been their custom for a number of years to host a huge Calgary Stampede breakfast, the largest community-driven Stampede breakfast entirely run by volunteers (as is everything the Ismailis do). They had become used to feeding four to five thousand people, but this time they wanted to make the event even larger. Because the Aga Khan was coming, they rented the largest tent in North America and had it shipped from Florida. But when they erected it, before they were able to get it staked properly, a sudden windstorm caused it to collapse. They were lucky no one was killed. The tent was irreparable, and soon thousands of people would be turning up for breakfast. So between 3 and 6 A.M., the volunteers moved the entire operation two kilometres away to a parking lot. Volunteers were dispatched to guide the traffic to the new site and by 8 A.M. they were serving pancakes—five minutes later than promised. They fed more than six thousand people that day.

Naheed's brother-in-law has worked as a volunteer for three three-year terms, while Naheed used to put in forty or fifty hours a week. In addition to this, most Ismailis regularly attend meetings and social events at the jamatkhana. There are services every day. Growing up, Naheed didn't realize that most Christians attend church only on Sundays; Ismailis pray several times a day, and very devoted Ismailis go and pray in congregation twice a day, every day. Naheed himself goes to a service on Tuesday evenings and is in and out in thirty minutes. "Quick set of prayers, hello, goodbye," he laughs. Friday prayers can be even shorter. Some people stay for a sermon, some don't, and some stay for another service.

The faith of Ismailis like Naheed is braided into their everyday life; it is not a "Sundays only" deal. There seems to be something very practical about God's presence among them, and at an Ismaili wedding I recently attended, I observed that same feeling. There was a warm sense of community about the ceremony. The spiritual and the material are entwined. It's very different from the Christian tendency of separating the sacred and setting it in opposition to the secular. There is something integrated about Ismaili lives. A lot of it has to do with volunteerism as the lived expression of their faith.

The Aga Khan and his network of volunteers throughout the Third World—and now through his new Global Centre for Pluralism in Ottawa—accomplishes astounding work. He asks people to give up their jobs to carry out projects, and they do. Nurjehan Mawani, for example, was a high-ranking civil servant in Ottawa, chairperson of the Immigration and Refugee Board and a Public Service commissioner after that. In 2005, she was asked to go to Kyrgyzstan to develop a diplomatic presence there for the Aga Khan, and she's still there after six years. I first thought it was astonishing that someone would abandon such a high-powered career, but the Aga Khan Foundation tends to seek out people at points in their lives where a change like that makes sense or might be welcomed. Naheed says he is unlikely to be asked to relinquish his position as mayor of Calgary.

For most Ismailis, family comes first, and it's no different with Naheed. He considers his family's history to be "a beautiful story." Beautiful, even though it involves loss, displacement, and misunderstanding.

Naheed's own story began in East Africa, in Tanzania. But years before, his maternal grandmother came from a village in India, where she spoke Kutchi (an Indian dialect) and Punjabi. She was put on a boat and sent to be married to a man much older than her, a man who had already emigrated to Tanzania. She had ten children with him, and one of those children, Naheed's mother, married into another family of ten children. Many others had died in childbirth. They were poor, but they got along, working in a small shop and doing anything to stay alive and bring up their children.

Naheed's paternal grandfather died when his father was only eight years old, so his grandmother used to make food and sell it on the street. Eventually, the extended family moved to Arusha, a larger town in Tanzania, where they ran a small hotel. Arusha was a centre for a lot of UN activity, and Naheed's parents met some Canadians who worked for the Canadian International Development Agency (CIDA) and got the *Toronto Star* mailed to them. When they were finished with the newspaper, they would pass it on to Naheed's parents. And in 1968, his father saw pictures of the new City Hall in Toronto, designed by Viljo Revell, two semicircular shapes embracing each other. He was astounded by this piece of architecture; he didn't know how a building could be so tall and also so round. So he vowed that someday he was going to see it.

In 1971, the family gathered enough money together to make a trip to England, because his father's sister was getting married there. Her family had managed to save enough to send her to secretarial college in London. Once in England, Naheed's father was so determined to see Toronto's City Hall that they took off for Canada. At that point, Naheed's mother was pregnant with him, but they decided to go anyway. They arrived in June 1971. Decades later, when Naheed was sworn in as mayor of Calgary, he was allowed to have anybody he wanted to perform the swearing-in ceremony. Some people pick famous politicians, but he picked his sister, who told the story about his father and Toronto's City Hall and how, in a way, that led to the point where Naheed was now.

Obviously, Naheed's father was looking out for his family, because things were not going well in Tanzania. It wasn't as bad as Uganda, where Idi Amin was insanely attempting to eradicate the whole Asian population. But in Tanzania, President Julius Nyerere was applying the socialist principles of *ujamaa*—in many ways an idealistic attempt to abolish discrimination based on ascribed status, decentralize production down to the village level, and emphasize self-reliance through the group. This vision did not seem to include the country's Asian population, however, though much good was accomplished in vital areas of social development like infant mortality, education, and literacy. The Asian community saw that their rights were being taken away, that they were being marginalized and disenfranchised, and that their citizenship would disappear. A minority within a minority within a minority is always aware of any threat, and the Nenshi family saw no future for themselves in East Africa.

The Nenshis liked Toronto. They had a wonderful summer in 1971 and decided they would try to stay. Back then, it was possible to apply for permanent residency status after arriving in Canada. When they decided to do that, the Tanzanian government froze their assets at home and they were not allowed to take anything out of the country. All they had with them was their holiday clothes, and they weren't allowed to work. They lived in a rooming house and had several terribly difficult months, but luckily there was the kindness of strangers. At the time, there were only ten Ismaili families in Toronto, so they banded together and tried to help each other out. The longest any of them had been in Canada was one year.

Naheed's father decided that since he had run a hotel in Tanzania, he would try to get that kind of job here. He went to apply at the Inn on the Park, a large hotel north of the city. To get there, he took the Don Valley Parkway, but he ended up driving the wrong way on the expressway, and in a panic abandoned the car and started up the median on foot, with four lanes of traffic on either side of him. He presented himself for the interview covered in snow. He didn't get the job.

When applying for permanent residency status, there was a very simple way in which people could help each other. In order to get status, it was necessary to have a certain amount of money in the bank. Among Naheed's community (and probably among many other communities), the same amount of money, which various people had pooled together, was circulated between different bank accounts, so that when immigration officials checked, the money was there. It was done on a basis of total trust, and at the end the money was divided up again. Legally speaking, I'm sure this would be looked on as bending the rules, but what if you were in the same position? Most Ismailis could not return home without being persecuted or starved out, so, because they trusted and helped each other, they were able to arrive at this creative solution.

Naheed was the first in the Nenshi family to be born in Canada. His parents couldn't return to Tanzania; there was nothing to go back to. They had only high school educations, but Naheed characterizes them as being "very, very, very smart." People from minority groups do tend not only to develop intellectual abilities but also to become what my father called, in his 1920s slang, "quick on the uptake." And Naheed's parents knew that they would have to forge a future for themselves and for their children. They worked as junior office clerks and were able to call on their experience of running and managing hotels.

Soon after they arrived in Canada, the Asians from Uganda were accepted, and very quickly the tiny Ismaili community of a dozen families became a community of one thousand. So the ten families that had got here first had to help sort everything out for the people who came later. One of their members worked for CP Rail; that was a foot in the door. Now they could get jobs there for other Ismailis.

Naheed was living with his parents and sister in a small apartment in a high-rise with his uncle and his family: a total of two couples and four kids, in two bedrooms. But the family always maintained a spirit of adventure. After all, they were young, and they were alive and healthy and out of East Africa. They decided they would find more opportunity in Alberta, and that to get there they would drive across the country. They packed up their Dodge Dart and set off, with probably no idea how far it was. They set out in 1972, not really knowing what their prospects were, not knowing if they would ever see their families from Tanzania again, but with the hope that things could be better and the knowledge that they must make a start. Naheed remembers how they would save up to make long-distance phone calls to Tanzania. His family was lucky, because they all ended up in Toronto and Calgary. His mother's sisters all eventually settled in Calgary, and her four brothers moved to Los Angeles. Naheed's father worked as a bookkeeper in a company that made boxes, and his mother worked in the office of an appliance company. But they were entrepreneurs, like many Ismailis. So, with the little bit of money that they saved, they bought some real estate in Alberta, and in partnership with some other Ismaili families and friends started buying motels in very strange, small places such as Marble Falls, Texas.

When Naheed's family and friends bought a motel in Red Deer, Alberta, his parents quit their jobs and moved there. Although it was a small town, they thought they had a big opportunity.

The idea of the Nenshis going to Red Deer resonated with me, because I had learned in 2001 that the immigration and settlement committees of Lacombe and Red Deer were very active in welcoming immigrants. I paid an official visit to Red Deer, where I met new Canadians from eighteen different countries. They told me that at first they had worried about coming to a small town (Red Deer has a population of about fifty thousand), but its smallness turned out to be an advantage. It was easier to make friends in the larger community and to become familiar more quickly with details of Canadian life than it would have been in a city of millions. Their stories were overwhelmingly positive, whether they were Chinese, Filipino, Pakistani, or Croatian. One of our first programs for the Institute for Canadian Citizenship was inaugurated in Red Deer with enthusiastic co-operation from the city's officials, Red Deer College, and many of the new Canadians I first met there.

Naheed's family was part of that movement of immigrants beyond the large cities. But unhappily the recession of the early 1980s and interest rates of twenty-two percent nearly sank them. After about three years in Red Deer, they returned to Calgary and started again from scratch, even though they had become landlords of several properties by then. They managed to hang on to one property, but the rest were gone on foreclosure. They moved back into their old house in Calgary. Naheed's mother got a job first as a chambermaid in a hotel that was owned by people they knew. Saving a bit, his parents bought a small laundromat. When Naheed was thirteen years old, he worked the counter at the laundromat and did his homework while minding the cash and selling detergent and fabric softener. His father went back to work at the box company in a more junior position and eventually found himself working for his sister. He stayed on there until he retired. His mother also worked in Marlborough Mall, selling lottery tickets at an information booth. She was doing really well, but the entrepreneurial bug kept biting her, so they decided to open their own little lottery booth in a grocery store, eventually adding more. Later they sold them, but Naheed's mother continued to work at a lottery booth until she retired.

Naheed thoroughly enjoys telling the story of his resilient family and their attempts to be entrepreneurial. The family was on unemployment insurance for a while in the early 1980s when there was absolutely no income. Naheed knows what it is to depend on that very basic guarantee that can keep you from total destitution. He says they never indulged in self-pity because they could always see that there was someone worse off than them.

Naheed says his parents worked hard to ensure their children went to university. They didn't dream that he would go to university: they required him to go. It was not an option. It was for this that they worked all the time. They loved their children, but they depended on them to have initiative. And the children knew that their parents had a goal for them.

Naheed grew up in the area of east Calgary known as Marlborough, which he describes as a diverse community, not in terms of race but of class. Back then, working-class people and people in trades did quite well economically; they could afford a boat and a cottage. While he was in school, the neighbourhood changed as Vietnamese boat people began to arrive. It was mostly a pleasant neighbourhood, with decent-sized single-family homes, big trees, a lot of recent immigrants. He calls it a typical suburban upbringing. Over the years, the community became more ethnic. Naheed still lives near Marlborough, but a little farther northeast. He says, very modestly, he's done rather well with some investments, so he made a deal with his parents that they would sell the house, buy a new one, and he'd pay for the difference so they could live mortgage free. It's clear that he still belongs to his family and wants to be part of it economically and emotionally—one of the beautiful things about his immigrant experience.

While he worked his way through university, Naheed always had at least three or four part-time jobs, and since Grade 6 he has worked in various family businesses. He served coffee in a bingo hall where everybody was white. All the other employees were children of people who played bingo, and they made up a shifting community. They'd work for two or three months and then move on, but Naheed stayed for three years. He insists that it's his immigrant mentality that made him stick to the job for three years.

I asked Naheed if the people at the bingo hall ever made him feel second-class or treated him badly. He said they never talked much to him, but they weren't cruel or hateful. Even so, they emphasized the difference they felt by giving him a funny nickname. They didn't mean anything by it, he says. I found it significant that Naheed did not say the nickname aloud. I think in fact it probably isn't something he can shrug off and make fun of. He describes it in a very interesting and self-protective way: he says it was their way of "observing the world." He remembers that at the time there was debate about whether Sikhs in the RCMP should be allowed to wear turbans. He would sell lottery tickets to nice old ladies wearing protest pins depicting a Sikh in a turban with a big X through it. Those ladies would think nothing of buying a ticket from him and then inviting him to coffee. Naheed regards this as a kind of interesting dichotomy. He doesn't think of it as anything profound or anything that couldn't change. And, indeed, in this specific case things did change. Sikh members of the RCMP not only wear turbans, they wear them during the iconic Musical Ride. All that was needed for this idea to lose its novelty was time.

Naheed ran for president of the student council in high school and won, he says, because "I'm pretty outgoing." Later, he was part of the team that won the provincial debating championships and placed eighth at the world championships. He played Oberon in *A Midsummer Night's Dream*. Every year, he served on student council. He insists that he was one of the nerdy kids as opposed to the popular kids, and when they had a party at graduation, he realized the nerdy kids outnumbered the popular ones. He loved high school. He went to Queen Elizabeth High, and he says that many people from the school volunteered to help him when he ran for mayor. People he would not have expected, those "popular kids," were coming out on Facebook saying what a great guy he was. He says he never suffered teenage angst; he just had a great time and a splendid university experience. He loved the idea of being with people who were completely different. As president of the student council, he tried to set up a new national student lobbying organization, and he managed to get himself flown to Toronto and be interviewed for a job at McKinsey at the same time. He got the job at McKinsey, and the rest is history.

2

Nadir Mohamed

When he was a little boy in Tanzania, Nadir Mohamed thought the greatest treat in life was a Coca-Cola with salted peanuts in it. Now he is one of the most powerful business leaders in Canada—the president and chief executive officer of Rogers Communications, the company that makes so many of our connections with other Canadians. A thin, energetic fifty-four-year-old at the top of his game, he too comes from the 1972 exodus from East Africa. A chartered accountant and an outsider, he has become the dynamic figure in an industry that requires insight, imagination, and prescience. The Ismaili community is proud of the way he has come to the top, and he feels that his business acumen has been fortified by that community's ethics.

He has interesting insights into the way in which people in his Ismaili community interact with each other. As the Ismailis have been dispersed around the world since the thirteenth century, they have become used to living in different countries and operating on many different levels at once in culture and in language, speaking not only their own language but also that of the community they have been dispersed to. Looking back on his home life when he was a child in Tanzania, Nadir says they spoke, interchangeably, English, Kutchi, Punjabi, and some Swahili. What's fascinating about the way these languages were spoken, he says, is that you knew instinctively to whom you would speak in which language. To his mother, he generally spoke Kutchi; with his grandmother, there were usually some words of Swahili; and with certain friends they would speak in a mixture of English, Punjabi, or Kutchi. With his father, he generally spoke English.

This ability to live with linguistic complexity is something many immigrant groups bring to Canada, but perhaps none in such a rich context as that of the Ismaili people. To switch back and forth in languages between generations and friends, between father and mother, is to develop a consciousness of differences and a sensitivity to people. It reminds me of Hong Kong in the early 1960s, when I spent time there visiting my father. I was very interested in the way people could sit at a dinner table and shift easily from English to Shanghai dialect, to Cantonese, and then to Mandarin. There was no hierarchy accorded the languages spoken: they were interchangeable. It seems to me that immigrants who come with more than one language from their country of origin can help Canada understand our need for bilingualism. I don't think they feel left out because the official languages are English and French; I think they are more sophisticated in their attitudes towards languages and that complexity is something they welcome. When you look at enrolment in French-immersion schools in Canada (which provide schooling for more than three hundred thousand students), you see that the children are as ethnically diverse as the population in general. Newcomers to this country regard French and English as levers to get the best jobs and compete with others on the same footing. Immigrants can help us continue to keep our country bilingual because they understand the value of speaking more than one language. Whether they are from Asia or China or Africa, they know that the more ways you can communicate with people, the better you understand them and the more you can control your own life and your destiny.

Nadir's father was a merchant with a hardware shop selling construction materials and building supplies, which he had built up from a very small business. After all the employees had gone home, Nadir, his mother, and sister would sometimes sit with his father while he prepared the accounts from that day's transactions. He was always aware of how much work went into building a small business, of how hard his father worked. The way he talks about it makes you feel he was implicated in working hard, that the whole family was part of the effort. In school, they mixed with Africans, but a great deal of their life was spent interacting with other Ismailis.

From the mid-1960s on, the Mohamed family, like many other Ismailis, began to plan for a future that would mean leaving Africa. The Ismailis had been in East Africa for several generations, but they knew they were outsiders, particularly since Idi Amin began his persecution of Asians in Uganda and since Tanzania adopted policies that favoured its African citizens over its Asian ones. Nadir's family began to consult friends and business associates about where he and his sister could be educated. They considered education to be a global passport, which, once acquired, could never be taken away. Nadir was sent to England to be educated, with the long-term view that the whole family would someday live somewhere else.

During the three years Nadir spent at boarding school in England, his family moved from East Africa to Vancouver. He was just a young teenager, alone and far from home, and although it might sound heart-wrenching and difficult, he insists that he enjoyed it. He could enjoy his independence and play as much cricket and tennis as he wanted. (Of course, being part of the British colonial tradition, the games for a young boy were the same, whether in East Africa or East Anglia.) When I speak with people who have come from countries that were once colonies of Britain, I identify with their sense of security, because my parents also felt that way coming to Canada: the postboxes were red; words were spelled the same. Perhaps it's a sense of emotional infrastructure, which is the good side of colonialism, and my family found it when they were uprooted from Hong Kong and found refuge in Canada.

The young Nadir had the luxury of spending holidays on his own in a flat in London, semi-supervised by a relative in his twenties, which was something of a dream for a teenager. I'm always struck by the fact that young people remember things in a very matter-of-fact way. Whatever happened, happened. His parents rented the flat for him, and at the age of fifteen he was living there. It was small, with two single beds, but he didn't have to pay the rent. It suited Nadir, but he now realizes that his parents thought it would be better to go somewhere other than England, and because of the Aga Khan's arrangement with Pierre Trudeau, Canada would be their destination.

The Mohameds picked Vancouver mainly because of its weather. When people say that they moved to Vancouver because of the weather, I always remember that my mother, in the 1940s and 1950s, used to mutter that she would like to move to Vancouver, where she knew she could grow rhododendrons and where there was so little snow. But my father always said we would never live in British Columbia, and particularly not Vancouver, because they were so prejudiced against the Chinese—and look what they'd done to the Japanese Canadians during the war, to people who had been born there. It was so drummed into me that we couldn't go to British Columbia, I didn't visit Vancouver until I was thirty and had worked in television for five years.

At the time when the Mohameds settled in Vancouver and Nadir joined them there, the Ismaili population was fewer than fifty people, maybe twenty families, who came from that part of East Africa with Somali, Muslim, and Indian heritage. After finishing high school in Vancouver, Nadir went to the University of British Columbia, where he met other Ismailis and there was a natural sense of community. And like all Ismailis, they believed in being citizens of the place where they were, wherever they lived. The lesson the Ismailis have to teach us in Canada is that they don't just stick together, they try to become a part of the other, a part of the larger world in which they have found themselves, to which they can contribute.

Initially, of course, the first priority was the Ismaili community, where they would help support newcomers. They created institutions that would help Ismailis settle, help seniors deal with social issues, or help people wanting to start businesses.

As Governor-General, I used to travel across the country to give out the Caring Canadian Awards and formally recognize people who volunteered. The youngest recipients in that time were two teenagers from Calgary, a brother and sister, who were Ismailis. I realized then how much that ethic of volunteering is a part of Ismaili life. I can understand groups helping each other within the group, but the Ismailis have made a point of involving themselves in other communities as well. This has been the successful element in Naheed Nenshi's appeal to the people of Calgary. At the age of thirty-eight, he knows what it is to give back to his community, because he has been giving back to it since he was a very young person.

Nadir Mohamed thinks that when you move from country to country or from continent to continent, there's a natural sense of "how do we settle and make the best of where we have come to?" The Ismailis have had the great fortune of being led by the Aga Khan, who speaks about the values of contributing to society in a practical as well as spiritual way. He says that we are all one creation, no matter where or who we are in the world, and that this helps us realize we are all responsible for each other.

People who have been forced to move, either because of persecution or exclusionary discrimination, quickly appreciate what it means to settle. They learn how to integrate and be part of different communities. Volunteering helps them gain control of their lives in the best possible way, by giving of their time and making personal commitments. And this control leads to advancement, not only in their personal development, but also in the broader community, where individual contributions, if they are significant, are recognized by others.

Volunteering also means learning to work with different kinds of people, to reconcile different points of view. The reward is the achievement of a shared goal. Of course, the task at hand, whether it's organizing a campaign to eliminate a certain disease or to raise money for a community centre, is always a goal. But when people volunteer, a different kind of dynamic develops, and this can become a great training ground for leadership, a superior kind of leadership that provides an ethical framework for social activity. Nadir says that it helps you visualize where you want to be in three or five years; he adds that volunteering has helped him in his corporate life because it, too, involves dealing with others and always having the greater good in mind.

Nadir remembers being interviewed for a high-ranking job and being asked who his mentors were, whom he looked up to. His instinctive first answer was his mother. He picked his mother because she always thought about perspective and context, although she would never have put it that way herself. But he knew that if she saw somebody who had done something wrong, her first instinct was not to condemn or shun that person but to think about what had caused them to behave as they did. This generous view led Nadir to conclude that you can be helpful if you understand a person's context for doing whatever he or she does. This is where the world of volunteering leads to an ability to understand the other in a profound way. He feels that he was blessed to learn that. He was never told it, he just observed it as he grew up. His admiration for his mother continues, because to this day people tell him about things his mother did for others. She instilled in him the belief that everybody has a story, and if you knew it, you might be able to understand them. And if you understood them, you could actually get around to solving and helping.

When Ismailis like Naheed and Nadir speak to me about volunteerism and giving back to the larger community, I think they are doing today what the social gospel movement, born out of evangelical Christianity, did in the early twentieth century in Canada. Then, members of various churches secularized the values of their religion to help remedy the ills of modern industrialized society. In the Ismailis' attempt to bring ethical value to everyday life and relationships between people, I see a resonance with the way they give of themselves. They seem to take the same optimistic view of human nature—mutual caring, responding to need—that motivated the social gospel movement from which people such as J.S. Woodsworth and Tommy Douglas sprang. We have welcomed into our midst people who combine deep spiritual belief about the connectedness of human beings with social action, which has practical results for the world around them. This group of Muslims, in effect, has given new energy to one of the long-standing aspects of the Canadian character—the desire to reach out and help others.

When I went to Ottawa in 1999, I was told that twenty-five percent of Canadians were volunteers, and the Governor-General's Caring Canadian Award, inaugurated by my predecessor, Roméo LeBlanc, was instituted to recognize those who gave of themselves in this way. The presence of approximately one hundred thousand Ismailis whose ethos is volunteering will help immeasurably to keep this Canadian trait vital.

His father emphasized hard work, and Nadir feels that together with his mother's concern for others, his parents gave him the real basis for the brilliant career he has subsequently enjoyed. He feels that the complexity of his Indian, East African, Islamic background brought with it advantages that outweighed the fact that his family was uprooted. He emphasizes again and again the energy, commitment, and love that his parents put into their children, so that they could be educated, and so that they could feel they were capable of anything. He realizes that he was the product of two generations of terrific struggle and uncertainty, but that he and others of his generation have benefited from their parents' hard work and sacrifice.

I identify very much with Nadir Mohamed's interpretation when I say that my family arrived with one suitcase per person. I should add that they also carried in them the notion that they could survive. My parents had a tremendous belief in their children, who were then only six and two and a half. I felt that my parents would have cleaned gutters, mopped floors, been short-order cooks, washed dishes in a restaurant if it meant a bright future for my brother and me. It was the underlying knowledge of this (and this is what I sensed in Nadir Mohamed's words) that has given me the strength to continue to build on something. I have had the solid foundation of their beliefs and their dreams and their hard work.

When I first asked him to talk to me about his early life for this book, Nadir said he really didn't see himself fitting in, because his life had not been a struggle. But I think I convinced him that he had built his life on top of a struggle. This is what I feel about my own life. That all I had to do was persevere. My mother didn't go out to work the way Nadir's mother did, but she scrimped and saved for us to eat good meals and to occasionally make beautiful birthday cakes with green and violet icing. Our parents didn't believe that they were sacrificing; they were simply living their lives to make sure that their children's lives would be better. It sounds so simple, and yet it was such a struggle. When it was accomplished, it was as though it was always meant to be.

Both Nadir's parents and mine had everything taken away from them. Mine by war and his by the rules of Tanzania, because when they left East Africa they were not allowed to liquidate any financial assets. His father, having owned his own business, realized he couldn't just go and work somewhere, because he'd never worked for another person before. In Canada, he got into the motel business with his brother, while Nadir's mother worked in a factory.

We discussed colonialism: how the British Empire had divided its peoples and transported them around, and how they handled them once they'd got to certain places. In Hong Kong, for example, the Indians owned the textile stores and were valued as police. There was a sense that somehow there was a master plan in which different colonial groups were used to limit and control others. Those of us who have that in our background understand that complexity—and perhaps, depending on where you came from, subconsciously resent being controlled and manipulated. Canada is a place where those edges cease to matter and where we all blend into one another. I have seen that happen in my lifetime, and it has persuaded me that human nature does not have to be about dividing, separating, and choosing sides. All those people, whether from Hong Kong or Uganda or Tanzania or India, can be part of a fabric that is woven together. The idea of settlement and then, after two or three generations, resettlement makes one anxious to create a community that cannot be broken up, that gets larger and larger, that becomes the circle considered by the Aboriginal peoples to be the shape of human connection.

What is it about Canada that allows people like the Ismailis to flourish? This is the question many who have succeeded ask themselves. They know that it isn't that they succeeded against all odds, but that the odds were not against them. This is something that I recognize in myself. I succeeded; there were difficulties, but the odds were not against me. That is what Canada has done for us.

THE BLUE TATTOO,
THE BLUE CANDLE

When I was ten years old in Ottawa, I used to get my chocolate Mello-Roll ice cream cone on Thursdays—a once-a-week treat. One day, as the woman serving me handed me my nickel change, I saw that on the back of her hand there was a tattooed number. The number rippled with the veins across the skin. I never mentioned it to my parents, or to my beloved teacher, Miss McRae, at Elgin Street Public School. I never mentioned it because I think I didn't really want to understand what it meant. I had never seen anything like those numbers, and the word "tattoo" was unknown to me then. It was only years later that I came to connect those tattooed numbers with the unspeakable horror of concentration camps. The idea that there were people in Canada who were survivors of this was hard for me to imagine. I didn't put it together until well after I'd seen movies about the Nazis and the Holocaust.

Canada accepted many people who were displaced after the Second World War. Girls and boys would arrive in Grades 5, 6, and 7 who didn't speak a word of English and came from unspecified places in Europe, where they had lost everything because of the war. Somehow, I didn't feel there was a great difference between them and me. After all, my family had arrived less than ten years before. We heard the words "displaced people," or "DPs," a lot, and I remember one of my mother's friends saying she didn't understand the attitude that it was somehow *their* fault that they were displaced. We all knew about the war and how the boundaries of countries had shifted, and that people of those countries were the victims. It was one thing that our family never felt—that we were victims. We always felt we were better than, or at least as good as, the people of our adopted country.

The policy of the time was that displaced people would be accepted in Canada if they spent a year either in agricultural or domestic work. My parents told me that many of these people had come from much better circumstances than they were finding in Canada, which my mother, in her worst mood, would characterize as "rustic" or even "crude." I remember her coming back from a cocktail party in a very fashionable part of town and telling me that she had spoken at length with the family's maid, who had beautiful blond hair that was cut very short. The woman was Hungarian. She had been in the Hungarian National Ballet in Budapest, but when she came to Canada, her employer had made her cut her hair short. I knew my mother identified with her. When I grew older, I met a Romanian princess who had spent her first year in Canada on a pig farm in Saskatchewan. And one of the plant nurseries in Ottawa was cultivated by a Baltic nobleman and his Russian princess wife with whose daughter I later went to university. It was a time of mixed and adjusting values, a time of reassessment of status, a time of surprise and survival.

But those numbers on the back of that woman's hand always haunted me. In January 2005, I went to the sixtieth anniversary of the liberation of Auschwitz. It is roughly sixty-five kilometres from Krakow, Poland. More than thirty heads of state were gathered there to represent their countries. I sat in minus-ten-degree weather on open bleachers with the Queen of the Netherlands, the King of Norway, Vladimir Putin, and others. We travelled there together by bus rather than by train. It occurred to me then that surely the rail lines leading into Auschwitz could have been bombed by the Allies as soon as they learned about the exterminations. I know there is much debate among historians about why this didn't happen; some say that Churchill tried to do it but was let down by his bureaucracy. That the Nazis' ruthless campaign of extermination could have been stopped, or at least slowed, by destroying the means of bringing people to the furnaces is a moral question with which I hope we will always torture ourselves.

That day had begun in a theatre in Krakow with a moving eyewitness account, via video from Moscow, from the liberating officer, then nearly ninety years old. Major Shapiro of the Red Army had liberated Auschwitz in the same way Canadian and British soldiers liberated Belsen.

Later, at Auschwitz, it was damp and freezing, and there were snow flurries. There were official representatives from some fifty nations. But most important, the survivors of Auschwitz were there with their families, several thousand of them, filling the flat centre ground in front of the ceremonial platform. When everyone was seated, the speeches began. As soon as President Katsav of Israel had finished his speech, he was rushed by a woman dressed only in a white T-shirt and flimsy trousers. She addressed him in Polish, and we came to realize that this interloper was actually a survivor. (Some people came to translate for us when it was obvious she was not going to be taken away.) She said she'd been in the camp as a young teenager, and that through all the time they were attempting to survive, their clothing was no warmer than what she was wearing now. It was a moment of high drama. President Katsav stood there at a total loss while security men milled around in confusion. Eventually, after ten very long minutes, she withdrew from the stage and the ceremony proceeded.

Each country's representative was given a lighted candle in a blue glass holder, and when our country's names were called, we were to proceed to the platform and lay it in front of the Auschwitz memorial. I noted, as I was called for Canada, that the dignitaries, all dressed respectfully in black, had been joined at the last minute by a man in a khaki army anorak with "USA" embroidered on the left shoulder. It was U.S. Vice-President Dick Cheney. When I placed the candle on behalf of Canada in memory of all who had perished at Auschwitz, I was thinking of the lady in the variety store with the tattoo on the back of her hand.

In the course of my long television career, I met many survivors of the Holocaust and of the war. In 1994, when I was producing *Adrienne Clarkson Presents*, a man called George Brady came to see me with a manuscript containing children's poems, letters, and drawings. This remarkable person (who recently celebrated his eightieth birthday) had been a child at Theresienstadt, the holding camp for concentration camps like Auschwitz. As a fourteen-year-old, he was brought from Prague to Theresienstadt with many other children separated from their parents. Theresienstadt was a "model" camp for Jews, shown off to the international community as a healthy place to keep undesirable people. Unfortunately, many people believed that to be acceptable at the time. As the children grew older, many of them were shipped off to the concentration camps, where they disappeared forever.

George and his friends were taught by some brilliant Jewish professors who gave them classes and encouraged Friday-night literary sessions, for which the children wrote poetry and short stories. Somehow, the writings had all been saved, and George wished to publish them and make them known to the world.

After the war, George himself was a displaced person. He came to Canada, and eventually started a plumbing business based on what he'd learned as a plumber's assistant in the camp. The business did well, and George was able to buy a house in Toronto and a cottage in Muskoka. He has subsequently become known as the brother of the eponymous heroine of *Hana's Suitcase*, the story of how his sister's belongings were shipped around the world and ended up in Japan after she perished at Auschwitz, which has became a very moving book and film.

When George came with his proposal to do a program, we decided we would go back with him to Theresienstadt and film him there and at Auschwitz and in Prague, where some of the other camp boys now lived. George had been brought up in a completely secular way, and until the Nazis arrived had thought of himself as more Czech than Jewish. But being swallowed into a vortex of anti-Semitism and persecution changed all that.

The children who were victims of the hideous indictment of our civilization now known as the Holocaust are among us as Canadians who have lived fruitful lives and contributed to the public good. Often we can know them for years before we hear their terrible stories. When I met Fred Bild, then Canada's youthful ambassador to Thailand, in 1980, I had no idea what he had lived through as a small child. After knowing him for twenty-five years, I learned from him about a survival and a transformation that changed not only his own life but ultimately the lives of thousands of others.

3

Fred Bild

As a small boy of nine who was reunited with his mother after two years of war, Fred Bild learned what family really means. Fred Bild has now retired from Canada's Department of Foreign Affairs, where he served all his career as a foreign-service officer and ultimately as a senior ambassador. As a Jewish child, he was taken up in a rescue network that spread from Brussels and Antwerp to the countryside, a network of devoted and risk-taking people who hid Jewish children from the Nazis. Just before the Second World War broke out, rallies were held and posters put up in Belgian towns exhorting citizens to take in Jewish refugee children soon after the persecution of the Jews became known. In the Jewish museum in Brussels today, you see evidence that meetings were organized by Protestant pastors and Catholic priests to encourage Belgians to help look after those children fleeing Germany.

Fred Bild was born in Leipzig in 1935. The family were furriers. They read the newspapers and were increasingly worried about the Nazi menace. It seemed to seep right into Fred's consciousness, even though he was only three years old at the time of the

1938 *Anschluss* in neighbouring Austria. He knew in his earliest
memories that there was somebody called Hitler and that he was
monstrous. Late in 1938, the family left Germany, and as young
as he was, Fred knew they were running away from something. He
remembers now that his mother came from the same part of Bavaria
where Henry Kissinger was born, and that Kissinger's father was
his mother's Jewish teacher. There were classes in religious instruction for Jews in Germany then, because all religions were tolerated.
Different religions had their own instructors, who came and taught
the children in school.

Although Fred's parents made a reasonable living, they were
by no means prosperous. Many people like the Bilds wanted to
emigrate to the United States, but they knew the process would
take too long—the paperwork, the waiting in bureaucratic offices.
Then Kristallnacht happened and they decided they had to leave
as soon as possible. They had been experiencing persecution for
quite some time and knew that to escape they would have to be
smuggled out of Germany. It probably meant accommodations
with people they didn't know, perhaps some money helped, and
by a combination of circumstances, they made it to Antwerp in
late 1938.

Like most refugees, Fred's family first found a place to stay
in the slums. Even at age three, Fred can remember his parents
wondering if they could stay in such a place, what would become
of them, and how they would live with no income. And then they
heard about a place called Marneffe, near the city of Namur; it was
a refugee camp set up by the Belgians to cope with the dramatic
influx of people from Germany. Fred later learned that the refugees
who had been passengers on the *St. Louis*—which had set out on
a tragically fruitless journey to freedom across the Atlantic and

been turned away by Cuba, the United States, and, shamefully, Canada—were in the camp at the same time.

As a child, Fred didn't find camp life difficult. There were other children to play with, and they had sand piles in the summer and snow in the winter to make snowballs and forts. The biggest problem was food: he didn't want to eat anything except the puddings they had for dessert. Fred vividly remembers his mother urging him, then scolding him, to eat. He had relatives in the camp, including a cousin who later emigrated to the United States and with whom he remains in close touch.

When war was declared in 1939, the Bilds were still in the Marneffe camp. It's a vivid memory for Fred because his father told him not to play outside, despite the fact that it was May and beautiful weather. When his father explained that there was a war, the four-year-old thought to himself, "What's a war?" He asked whether he'd be able to play outside tomorrow, and the answer was, no, probably not. And probably not after that. Little Fred began to realize that tomorrow was stretching out. The future appeared very, very long.

Planes were overhead when the refugees started to take to the road. After two days, they knew the Germans were on their heels. They formed that iconic image of war: a long line of people fleeing the enemy, carrying all their belongings in their small bags. Fred's father had sewn himself a rucksack, and each of his parents carried a suitcase as they dragged Fred along by the hand. They slept in the fields or in barns or stables. And yet Fred wasn't frightened when the planes flew over. He remembers Belgian soldiers sometimes mingling with the long file of people, and seeing for the first time a dead horse lying on the road. By age four, he already knew that people died or got killed; he used to play with toy soldiers, and they would kill each other. But he had never realized that animals died. Or that people would kill them.

His mother had brought a fur coat with her. She never wore it; she used it instead as a cover for them when they slept. She also flung it over them when they were strafed by planes and had to throw themselves on the ground. Fred couldn't understand why people lay on the ground at a time like that; he thought it made them a bigger target. He remembers this as a childlike thought about survival.

It took them about three weeks to get to the French border, and by then there were thousands of refugees. Belgians taking to the road had joined in. Even today, whenever you see a film or news report of refugees, they are always in those same lines, two, three, or four across in what seems like an endless ribbon of humanity, going from somewhere to something uncertain. Fred's group was eventually confronted by a German officer on horseback leading his men. He told them they had to go back, that they were only headed deeper into the fire. They realized then that the Germans were already in France; there was no point in trying to escape there. Back they went to the camp.

It was like rewinding a tape. They walked back through the same countryside, but this time there was no more fighting, and all of the farms were empty of people. Cows were mooing because nobody had milked them. Sometimes, one of the refugees would go and milk them. They would sleep in the empty houses, and the children were able to play with the abandoned toys.

When they got back to the camp at Marneffe, there was no longer anybody there to ensure food was coming in or to look after any of the basics they'd taken care of earlier. So his parents decided they would have to return to Antwerp, even though the Germans had occupied the country. During that winter, the Germans put in place a kind of pilot project for corralling male Jewish refugees. Fred's father was sent with others to Limburg province in Holland to cut down trees. Eventually, he was released and sent back to the camp, but by rounding up people like that, the Germans started to keep records. Everyone had to register, and everything was very carefully put down in some ledger, neatly and inescapably.

Antwerp was a small town with a concentrated Jewish community that worked in the diamond trade; they were living together in a de facto ghetto. Obviously, this became dangerous. So the Bilds decided to go to Brussels, where they wouldn't be as easily identified. This was just about the time that Fred would start school, as he was turning six that August.

The question of how to earn a living was a huge problem. The Depression lingered, and nobody seemed willing to employ his father. Jewish committees formed in each town, and they had a very small amount of money to share with members every week or every month. Fred remembers his parents talking about going down to get this pittance every week. His father remained jobless, but his resourceful mother found a wholesaler who supplied her with clothes and stockings to sell; she would peddle them to retailers and other people. She found this easier to do in Antwerp than in Brussels, and so she kept a little room in Antwerp where she'd spend two or three days at a time, peddle her goods, and return to Brussels with a little bit of money. Meanwhile, Fred's father took care of him as he began school and started to learn French. The language at home was German, but he didn't find it difficult to learn French.

One day, he came home to discover that his mother had not come back. She had been arrested in the street for staying out past the curfew. She spent six weeks in prison. His father decided he was going to visit her in prison and take Fred with him. They went to see the German commander in his office. There was a young officer there with a small sword, which deeply impressed Fred. The officer stared at them and said, "I can't stand the smell of this Jewish rabble."

When Fred recounts this now, he makes a point of saying it was his only direct contact ever with that kind of open, anti-Semitic hatred. And it came from a German officer. Fred didn't know what the word "rabble" meant, but he understood that it must be terribly insulting, because his father said to him, "Did you hear what he called us?" For the first time in his life, Fred felt sorry for his father. He wanted him to stand up to the officer, punch him in the face. One can only imagine that kind of feeling in a six-year-old who sees humiliation and who understands that nothing can be done except to swallow it.

In August 1942, Fred's parents returned to the house one day with yellow stars. They told Fred that they would have to wear them or be arrested. But many people asked, "What will they do to you if you *do* wear them?" A lot of their friends tried to have it both ways: they would put the star on their coat but carry the coat over their arm, so that if they were stopped they could say, "Well, I was wearing it." Fred wanted one even though his parents said, "Children don't need these." But Fred insisted, and when his mother bought him a new jacket, he made her sew on the yellow star.

About a month later, he went to visit a school friend and his parents went off to visit other friends. On his way home, he stopped at the apartment building where his uncle and family lived on the third floor. Fred's habit was to shout out to them and they would throw him down the key, but this time no one answered his call. Just down the street, people were talking excitedly. He put his coat over his arm so that the star wouldn't show, but a Belgian woman came up to him and told him that it was sticking out. She made sure he had folded his coat properly so it wasn't visible. When he got home, he let himself in with his key. Soon afterwards, a neighbour came and told him she had bad news for his mother: his father and uncle had been grabbed on the street outside the uncle's apartment building. They had been denounced by a Jewish collaborator. (Though long dead, this collaborator is still talked about in Belgium.) Fred has always believed that his father heard noises in the street, went out to see what was happening, and was spotted by German soldiers rounding up Jewish men. Even while rushing, his father had managed to latch the door to the building behind him, which meant that no one could go up and get anybody else. He was grabbed, and then he was gone forever. It was not until thirty years later that Fred learned for certain his father had been sent to Auschwitz and perished soon after.

Fred's mother was frantic with worry and tried desperately to find out where her husband had been taken. But she took the precaution of never sleeping in their apartment again. She went across the street and begged to be taken in by their neighbours. Until they found new lodgings, she and Fred slept in different places every night, finally ending up in a tiny little flat.

Adding to his mother's distress was the fact that she was pregnant. Fred learned that he was going to have a brother or a sister just as he lost his father. His mother had three sisters, two of them in Belgium with their families, and they huddled together trying to figure out what to do as, one by one, their husbands were taken away by the Nazis. One of the sisters was captured with her husband as the family fled to Switzerland. Their three little girls were left behind at a train station. Some Belgians found them and took them in, and later they ended up in the United States, where another uncle adopted them after the war.

Fred's mother was terribly worried; she and Fred now had a flat that was permanent. This meant that she had to register it as her address. And so she decided to send Fred into hiding, as she knew other people were desperately doing with their children. Fred was placed in the suburbs with a woman who was paid to keep children. His mother would come and visit him on Sundays. He remembers being very unhappy, and it was while there that he learned his cousins had all been shipped away. Fred was only in Grade 1, but he knew that Jews were being persecuted. He says now that it was perverse for him to see what was happening around him and think it was natural. But as Fred was telling me about this, I remembered my mother told me that when we were in Hong Kong, whenever bombs dropped and we were in one basement or another, I would clap my hands because I liked the sound of the bombs. Children adapt to everything. They are canvasses on which sensation, horror, and history can be written at the same time.

While his mother was terrified, she was also resourceful, and she managed to get them into a bigger apartment with her sister, who had lost her husband and two sons. They lived in an underground way, because his mother kept her tiny flat in Antwerp, where she got her mail. It was during this time, when Fred, his mother, and his aunt were living in the larger apartment, that his mother's labour began. She didn't want anyone to discover the rest of her family living in the apartment, so she took her suitcase and walked in the dark for fifteen minutes to the hospital. Later in life, she described this to Fred over and over in obsessive detail; it was the worst moment of her life. The nurses and doctors were professional and correct in their behaviour, but Fred's mother sensed that they knew about her situation and felt sorry for her. One of the nurses wept bitterly. They must have felt they were looking at a condemned person who was giving new life—but to what purpose? When his mother and the baby came home after ten days, Fred was disappointed; he had been expecting a playmate. Instead, his baby brother just slept, ate, and gurgled.

As they were living a clandestine life, Fred was not allowed to go to school because he would have to be registered. By August 1943, when his brother was about five months old, Fred was not allowed to play outside. Through a tiny crack in the window, they watched neighbours' houses as Belgian police, under German supervision, came and took people away. They knew that sooner or later they would be taken away, too. And although they had great faith in their landlord, his mother and her sister got in touch with the underground, people who sometimes left a small packet of ration stamps or sometimes money at their door. It helped keep their little family from starvation. Then his mother heard about a secret branch of the Red Cross. By negotiating with them, she arranged for Fred to be hidden, at a place unknown to her. Later, she would do the same for Fred's baby brother. Fred was her interpreter, because the woman from the Red Cross spoke only French. The woman assured Fred's mother that her son would be well looked after, and that he could write to her and the letters would be brought to her by intermediaries.

Fred remembers that he wasn't the least bit worried; his mother had saved him, and he was used to her doing that. When three young women came to take him away, he wasn't afraid. They all took the streetcar together. Though he may not have known it then, he realizes now that the women's good spirits were put on for his benefit, that they made a conscious effort to behave as normally as possible. They arrived at a cheerful castle. Fred entered a dormitory and then saw the classrooms, which were set up with little tables and chairs rather than desks. He remembers that the director, Mademoiselle Sorrel, looked at him and said, "J'ai pour lui une ferme où il mangera du pain blanc tous les jours." ("I have a farm for him where he'll eat white bread every day.") Fred was duly impressed. He hadn't ever eaten much white bread; all the bread he'd been getting in Belgium seemed to have sawdust in it, and it was dark and terrible. He waited at this castle home for several weeks, and the women were kind. Every night, all the children lined up to be kissed on the cheek by Mademoiselle Sorrel. Fred was renamed Pierre.

One day, Mademoiselle Sorrel was positively jubilant. She announced that the Allies had landed in Sicily (it was September 3, 1943). Fred knew that meant they would soon be liberated, but he didn't discuss this with the other little boys in his room whose fathers had been deported to labour camps or whose parents had fallen on very bad times. One after the other, the other boys went off to where Fred thought they might be eating white bread. Then finally, a young man of about eighteen came to Fred and said, "It's time. Now you'll go." The people at the children's refuge gave him a big apple and wished him bon voyage. He and the young man, whose name was Martin Aguirre, took the streetcar to Louvain, the apple bulging in the back pocket of Fred's knitted shorts. Martin told Fred that he should keep the apple and give it back to him at Malines. Then Fred took fright; he thought Malines meant the transit camp. So he ran away. He ran right past a German army garrison and the guard outside on duty, but he was finally caught.

He was taken screaming to the train station, and he felt his fate was sealed. Martin got him onto the train and explained to the other passengers that Fred had been at summer camp and was upset because he didn't want to go home.

They arrived at an exquisitely beautiful estate, and Fred realized it didn't look like a transit camp. It was, in fact, the mansion where the archbishop of Malines lived. Another priest living there was called Abbé Ceupens. The small boy and the two clerics had lunch together. He remembers that there were comic books. He had a splendid time, and a few days later Martin took him on a bicycle ride along the canals, where he saw beautiful houses and barges being pulled by handsome horses. He was taken next to a nunnery where the children of barge owners were left while their parents worked on the canals, and then a bearded priest came and took him to a village called Lubbeek, where he was put up in the local priest's house. Finally, when the bearded priest came back, he drove Fred to the farm where he would spend the rest of the war.

The farm belonged to eight brothers and sisters, none of whom had any children, and only two of whom had ever been married. So Fred turned out to be a kind of miracle child for them. He realizes now that they spoiled him. He was allowed to do anything he wanted, and they indulged him in any way they could. Even though these dour Flemish farmers were not, by nature, warm and friendly people, they were palpably affectionate towards him. They taught him how to clean out pigsties and cowsheds, and within six weeks he could speak Flemish perfectly (his German helped, of course). They brought books home from Brussels, not just school books but picture books and children's stories. Those people, who never spent a cent on themselves, bought him toys. The village priest came twice a week to give him school lessons.

The language they used was French, and after the war Fred found out it was a great sacrifice for the priest to do this, because he was a Flemish nationalist and wanted Flemish to be the language of Belgium. Two of the family members were nuns, one of whom was in a convent in Brussels and would come occasionally for weekends. The other would come sometimes to cook and sew for the entire family, and she was lovely to Fred. He considers it the most marvellous period: not only was he loved and taken care of, but he didn't have to go to school.

He remembers that on his first night there, they had a big discussion around him. He realized they were debating whether he should go out and work with them in the fields. No doubt they also discussed what kind of story they would tell to explain why they suddenly had a little boy in their midst. They settled on the story that he was one of those frail and sick children from the city, where there was nothing to eat, and that he was being taken care of in the countryside.

Every Sunday, he went to church and had to say his prayers— one of the nuns was very insistent on it. Her brothers paid lip service to the religion, but they swore and blasphemed with every breath. They wouldn't say prayers; they wouldn't light candles. Fred sympathized with them, because he didn't like the religious part very much, but he thought the brothers were unfair to their sister. Many Jewish children in his position were baptized as Catholics, but the family didn't do this to him. This caused a bit of a problem, because without being baptized, he couldn't receive communion and people might notice. But somehow that was fudged. He found the Latin mass boring, and there were no good tunes, but it was all part of their life, and he got used to it. He even imagined growing up to be a farmer.

Fred realized later that his new family was one of only two in the region to have taken in and sheltered Jewish children, and they did not know each other. It was a priest in Lubbeek who organized the operation, and he was a militant anti-Nazi. When he went on walks with the brothers, they would point out houses where they said collaborators lived. They told him sternly that they never spoke to the collaborators, and that nobody sat with them in church. Nobody ever said outright what they were doing to help the German occupiers; they were simply shunned. Fred is pretty certain that in that Flemish countryside nobody spoke to those people for the rest of their lives.

What Fred missed at this time wasn't love or attention. Curiously, what he missed was the tension, the feeling of living on the edge of catastrophe. At first, he was very worried about his mother and little brother, but since there was no news, he stopped worrying. Occasionally, there would be news about an uprising and killings in a nearby village. But there was no radio and there was no electricity in the village, except at the church and the school.

His adoptive family had somebody else living in the barn, Georges, who was a distant relative, and Fred kept him company in the barn during the daytime. Georges was in hiding because he had received orders to report for forced labour in Germany. One day, one of the neighbourhood girls beckoned to Fred and took him to her bedroom. She showed him a picture of Georges and asked if he had ever seen him. Fred said no, he had not, and walked out. Later, he learned that this was Georges' girlfriend, who wanted to know where he was hiding so she could see him; she suspected something, but Fred kept the secret and never told anybody.

Bombing raids by the Allies were getting more intense, and eventually the Germans started to leave, their trucks endlessly pouring east from all parts of Belgium. Their defeat was imminent. One day, in the spring of 1945, the family became aware that something was happening on the road far away. The land was flat, so Fred, who was the lightest, climbed up to the top of a huge pear tree, and from there reported that the Allies were on their way. The next day, Georges came out of hiding and went to visit his girlfriend. She pointed at Fred when she saw him and said, "That little guy there didn't give you away." Fred was considered a real hero.

In the weeks that followed, he couldn't believe what was happening; he would walk three or four kilometres to the main highway and just sit and watch the Allied trucks going by. He thought it was lovely.

Then one of the people who had helped bring him to Lubbeek went to find Fred's mother. He had written her letters, which were sent to the abbé in Malines, and the abbé would get someone in Brussels to deliver them to her door. Every couple of weeks, she got a letter from her little boy, but he never got anything back from her—it was too dangerous for him to be receiving any letters, and she had no idea where he was.

Eventually, she arrived at the village. It was a very traumatic moment for nine-year-old Fred: although he hadn't forgotten his mother, two years had passed and he had been very happy with his adopted family. But he did realize that in some way he was happy to see her. The worst thing was that now he'd have to go to school. His mother stayed for a couple of days and then left again to try to find his little brother, whom she had sent into hiding when he was ten months old. She told Fred he would have to stay where he was because she couldn't get ration stamps from the Resistance anymore and she had no income. She told him to be good and that she would come to visit him whenever he had holidays.

When Fred eventually rejoined his mother after the war, life in Brussels was a letdown; he missed farm life and his adopted family. He went back to visit them for Christmas and Easter and in the summers. Sometimes, he spent the whole summer with them, and he still felt very much that he belonged with them. He stayed in touch with them throughout his life until they all died. You can't help but feel that these people became Fred's true family because they provided stability and love instead of the tension and fear in which he had spent his early childhood. When he speaks of them, his eyes cloud with tears, and it's evident the emotion they aroused in him is something he will never forget.

He and his mother lived in Brussels until 1948. His little brother had been sent through the same network to the same chateau. In 1944, the Germans had requisitioned the chateau to house soldiers and were told they could do whatever they wanted to be rid of all the children. A German soldier who heard this jumped on his motorcycle and raced to the chateau to tell Mademoiselle Sorrel to get the kids out of there immediately. Mademoiselle Sorrel and her helpers took about fifty children, including tiny babies, on the streetcar in the middle of the winter east to Namur, where contacts provided them with another chateau. All of them, including Fred's brother, were saved.

When Fred's mother remarried, she and her husband decided they would emigrate to Canada, and Fred, at age twelve, was classified as a francophone. They came to Montreal, but because Fred was a Jew, he could not attend French school; you had to be Catholic to go to a French school. This is one point that Fred and I have in common: I wanted to go to a French school, and I couldn't because I was not a Catholic. It made me even more determined to learn French when I got older. If I couldn't learn French in Canada because I was Protestant, I would go to Paris when I grew up, which I did. Fred learned that Jewish children had to go to Protestant schools, so he was enrolled in a school in the Côte-des-Neiges area in Montreal, where he met a little girl called Eva Kornpointer.

Eva remembers Fred arriving in their class, a small boy who was very good in French but spoke little English. Fred declaimed poetry with gestures, and she saw how different he was. But obviously they always remembered each other, because when they met again at what is now Concordia University, when Fred was in his second year and Eva was in her first, Fred recognized her and said, "Hello, Eva Kornpointer!" She said, "Weren't we at school together in Grade 4?" And he said, "No, Grade 7, with Miss Henry." Fred made an enormous impression on her, and she says he has gone on impressing her daily for the last fifty-six years. They married when they were just twenty. He told her the story of his childhood soon after they met again, and whether that was one of the bonds that drew him to her and vice versa, they don't say, but I feel it must have been.

They graduated from university together and went off to England. They married almost as soon as they arrived, because they realized they were going to be together forever and so might as well. He went to University College London and she to the London School of Economics. Fred became very interested in international law and considered joining some kind of international organization, but he wasn't getting anywhere with the various letters he was writing, so he decided to apply to the Canadian Foreign Service exams at Canada House in London while Eva was giving birth to their first child. To their amazement, Fred was invited back to Canada to do the oral exam. He passed brilliantly, and they moved home in 1961.

Fred's career was dynamic, and he served in places like Laos and Paris before becoming ambassador to Thailand at the age of forty-four. Later, in Paris, he served as minister counsellor when Lucien Bouchard was our ambassador to France. Eva was responsible for helping Bouchard learn English by giving him daily lessons in his office. Bouchard had spoken only French until his appointment as ambassador. My term as Agent General for Ontario coincided with this period, and I was impressed by how quickly and well Bouchard learned English. At the time, he was well into his forties. Whenever anyone tells me they're too old to learn a language, I cite Lucien Bouchard's achievement.

Fred finished his career as our ambassador to China from 1990 to 1995. He made the news in an interesting way when he testified in 2009 to the Oliphant Commission that as ambassador to China he had accompanied Prime Minister Brian Mulroney to all his meetings there. Fred testified that there had been no discussion in China of the industrial investment that Mr. Mulroney had said he was working to promote and that was part of the reason he received cash payments from Karlheinz Schreiber. Fred now teaches at the University of Montreal, and on vacation he travels with Eva on a tandem bicycle in Europe. They recently completed an extraordinary trip around the world: avoiding airplanes, they travelled by bus, boat, and train into areas they had never been to before.

Growing up in Montreal, Fred was caught up in the language question in Quebec. He was forced to become an anglophone, first because he couldn't attend French elementary school, and later because he was turned away from the University of Montreal as he had not gone to *collège classique* and completed his *baccalauréat*. He says that he did not become a francophone again until he joined the Department of External Affairs, now Foreign Affairs.

The question of identity is fascinating in a person like Fred, because he was uprooted as a child and then virtually adopted by people so different from himself. Until the age of four, he grew up as a Jew, in a Jewish community, in a town in Germany. He feels that he is Jewish, but says, "I do not feel one bit religiously Jewish ... It's not there for me." He finds Judaism "interesting, but not a very attractive religion. It's interesting because so much literature is based around it, born through it." Perhaps because of his upbringing and because of his experience as a Canadian ambassador, Fred does not warm to things that are not inclusive. He believes that the most important thing to the Jewish people of his generation is their great achievement of survival. The survival itself forms their identity. He feels he has more in common with someone who has survived any kind of persecution than with someone who just happens to be Jewish. Fred went to a high school in Snowdon that was half Jewish, but felt he did not have much in common with his Jewish schoolmates, and none of them wanted to hear any of his stories. He feels they were not only not interested, but didn't know how to be interested. They had no idea how to understand it. Generally, he feels Holocaust survivors share his feeling: that people have no way of grasping what they went through.

Even though he was not a part of the Montreal Jewish community, there was one Jewish person who had a tremendous influence on him. His mother sent him to a B'nai B'rith camp in the Laurentians and William Shatner was his camp counsellor. His mother must have been quite shrewd, because she realized that he would do things in camp that he couldn't do in school; Shatner used to give him special lessons in English and had him act in a play. By the time September came along, after six weeks at camp, Fred was able to speak English fluently. He has never been in touch with William Shatner to tell him how important he was to him in his early life in Canada.

Fred feels his identity was shaped by the fact that he grew up in a series of situations of conflict: first, between Jews and their persecutors; then, living in Belgium, he was aware of the conflict between the Flemish and the Walloons, the French-speaking Belgians; and then, in Quebec, his Anglo and Jewish friends would make fun of the French, and he'd take the francophones' side. As a result, he has always been able to put himself in the position of the other person. This meant that when he became ambassador to Thailand, he was especially well equipped to deal with a situation that reminded him of his own thirty-five years earlier.

In 1975, Canada's Foreign Affairs department was grappling with the question of the Vietnamese boat people, who were leaving their country after the communists took control. Fred was appointed as ambassador to Thailand in the late 1970s, and he was told to hurry up and get there because the minister of foreign affairs of the new Conservative government, Flora MacDonald, was going to Geneva, and she wanted to make promises about how Canada was going to take care of the boat people. The shores of Malaysia, Singapore, Indonesia, Thailand, and the Philippines were being invaded by wretched, unseaworthy boats full of Vietnamese people who were trying to make their way through pirate-infested waters. It was hell on the sea, and these countries of first asylum weren't prepared to keep them. They said that if the Western countries didn't help, they would just push the boats back out to sea. Fred feels that they would have done it.

Minister MacDonald stated that the Canadian government would take in fifty thousand boat people (later upped to sixty thousand), and Canadians encouraged other settlement

countries—Australia, the United States, New Zealand, and France—
to do the same. Fred believes the British tried to weasel out of
making a commitment because they felt their position in Hong
Kong would make them unwilling recipients of hundreds of
thousands of refugees. Eventually, they took some refugees, but not
in great numbers. Switzerland didn't take in a lot of people, but
accepted problem cases, like the infirm. Fred assembled a group
of ambassadors from the receiving countries to monitor how the
United Nations High Commission for Refugees was doing its
work. The Canadian embassy in Thailand worked hard, and ended
up having the largest immigration section of any embassy in the
world at that time. Eight immigration officers spent all their time
going to the refugee camps and interviewing refugees. Wardair,
the airline run by Max Ward, provided charter planes, which the
Canadian government paid for in advance, and filled two planes
a month. Fred told his staff that it was their moral obligation to
fill those seats, that he didn't want a single one to be wasted. For
every seat that went back empty, there was a person who would be
unable to go. In many ways, Fred identified with the plight of the
boat people.

He feels that this was Canada's moment of greatest generosity.
All over the country, as you will see from John Tran's story later
on, small groups of people and individuals offered to take in the
refugees. In the end, more than one hundred and fifty thousand
Vietnamese refugees came to Canada. Eva and the Bild daughters
worked in the refugee camps, distributing clothes and other goods.
They also worked in the transit centres, which helped put families
back together, and performed other organizational duties.

As I sat with Fred in his comfortable, simple apartment in the
francophone area of Montreal known as the Plateau, I looked at

the picture of him and Eva when they were children, at the lovely pieces of Chinese porcelain and carved wooden chairs from their stay in China, and felt the atmosphere of lives truly lived in other places yet somehow made to blend with their own warm emotional life. I turned to Fred and asked him, "Do you ever wonder what would have happened to you if the Nazis hadn't come to power and there'd been no persecution and you hadn't come to Canada?" He laughed and touched his moustache and said, "Yes, I know what would have happened. I would have become a furrier in Leipzig."

PEOPLE ARRIVING
IN BOATS

Perhaps the single greatest emigration event to occur in the second half of the twentieth century was the exodus of the Vietnamese boat people in the late 1970s. Hundreds of thousands fled their country, mostly by sea, and one hundred and fifty thousand of them eventually made their way to Canada. There were virtually no Vietnamese in Canada before that, unlike the Chinese and Japanese, who had been here since the end of the nineteenth century, when they came to work as labourers. There was no familiarity in Canada with the Vietnamese, their language, their looks, or their food. They were known mostly for being from a distant country where the Americans had fought and been defeated. After the victory of the communist North Vietnamese, these people became known as the "boat people" because they began to flee their country in fragile, often unseaworthy, vessels and attempt to land in Thailand, Malaysia, the Philippines, and Hong Kong. In 1975, some 5,000 escaped, and by 1978 there were 3,600 people a month leaving Vietnam. The United Nations High Commission for Refugees (UNHCR) was desperately trying to resettle them. Canadians were inundated with images of Vietnamese boat people floundering in the South China Sea, beset by pirates. Their plight touched Canadians deeply. The most urgent problem was that the countries where the boat people were landing would not accept them unless the UNHCR helped find settlement for them elsewhere. They lived in make-do quarters wherever they could, often on the boats that had brought them from Vietnam.

I remember well the discussions many of us had about what could be done. Howard Adelman, a social activist in Toronto, worked very hard to get the refugees admitted to Canada. With public pressure building just before the federal election of 1979, Prime Minister Joe Clark's Conservative government agreed to accept fifty thousand of the desperate boat people. This was quickly blessed by Cabinet. Canada felt obligated probably because ten years previously we had been sensitized by the plight of the U.S. draft resisters. The Liberal government of the mid-1970s initially admitted two thousand Vietnamese people who did not have relatives in Canada. In addition, those who had relations here were allowed to come. In 1978, the communist Vietnamese government abolished "all trade and business operations of bourgeois tradesmen," which meant that the Vietnamese of Chinese ethnic origin, who owned the majority of small businesses in the country, were dispossessed. The Vietnamese government was worried the ethnic Chinese would be subversive, even though many of them had been in Vietnam for several generations. The estimates are that six hundred thousand people fled Vietnam, of whom nearly seventy percent were ethnically Chinese.

Meanwhile, something quite remarkable had sprung up. Groups and individuals in Canada came forward to sponsor the Vietnamese refugees, family by family. I remember people in my parish in Toronto sponsoring families, and hearing about others being sponsored by Jewish families and individuals. There were matching centres that put families and sponsors together, an overwhelming task, because sometimes the matching centre had to deal with passenger lists of up to six flights at any one time. The sponsors were asked to provide financial support for one year, averaging $2,500 per sponsor family. The money was meant to cover furnished lodgings, household goods, food, and clothing. The sponsor also undertook to counsel, transport, and help find employment for their sponsored family. This loose organization of sponsoring families across the country was dubbed Operation Lifeline, and to this day it remains an inspiring story from our collective social history. The core group members of the sponsoring families, as studies have shown, had university educations and combined family incomes of over $25,000, and many had travelled abroad.

When my family came to Canada in the middle of the Second World War, we knew hardly anyone who had a connection to Hong Kong. But through our public school and our Anglican parish, we met others who took a deeply personal interest in us. My brother and I were walked to school by people from a very old Ontario family, whom we had probably met through the church; we were invited to spend time with a Jewish pharmacist's family who lived in the neighbourhood. There was a sense, I believe, that people were looking out for us, even if there was no formal structure to do so. My father's job as a clerk in the Department of Trade and Commerce meant that he made friends among the other clerks, many of whom were French Canadian. We would have them over on Friday or Saturday night to play cards and chat, and they returned the invitations as well. This welcoming happened in a person-to-person way, and was not dependent on any social organization or civic structure. I guess this is what made me believe early on that Canadians basically do want to help other people when they are asked or when they see a need.

I was reminded of this when I was reading about a terrible snowstorm near Sarnia, Ontario, in December 2010. There was a full front-page photo of people who had been taken into Heather and Scott Helps' farmhouse after they had been stranded on the highway. The people in the photo included a Montreal truck driver, a couple trying to get to the airport for a trip to Germany, and a seventy-year-old man who had slept in his car the previous night. Mr. Helps had walked along the road in the snow, asking people in cars to come home with him. The stranded people stayed for several days with the Helpses until the snow was cleared. When someone is taken in because it is freezing outside, it is a spontaneous realization of the reality of that person's need, an identification with their plight as another human being.

One of my most moving tasks as Governor-General was to give out awards for bravery each year to about sixty or seventy people who have helped others, sometimes risking or losing their own lives to do so. Before I was in a position to meet these people and give them their awards (they would have been nominated by their communities, friends, and others, and their actions were well documented by public authorities), I somehow assumed that most people saved individuals who were known to them. But what I learned in the six years I was in Ottawa was that people will instinctively risk their lives to save others just because they wish to save a life. A recurring example of heroism: a person is driving down a four-lane highway and sees a car ahead of him start smoking, swerving, and pulling over to the shoulder. He follows and sees that this is obviously not just an ordinary car breakdown. He rushes to the car, attempts to pull the person out, sometimes with difficulty, sometimes even having to break through the windshield or the sunroof. Sometimes there is a baby strapped into the back seat. He gets the baby out as well. Seconds after dragging them to safety, the car is enveloped in flames. This is a fairly typical act of altruism that is not premeditated and is not part of any formal rescue activity.

The first time I encountered this, I was giving citations to eleven people from Saskatchewan who I assumed were members of a local volunteer fire brigade. In fact, they were just people having morning coffee at a highway café when somebody told them a truck down the road was in trouble. They all ran to pull the people from the truck, and minutes afterwards saw it blow up with such heat that the asphalt pavement melted and the highway had to be closed for several hours. After I heard about a number of these incidents, I asked a rescuer why he had taken such a risk. The answer was, "When I got to the car and I looked in at the driver, I thought, 'That person is me.'" In other words, his identification with the other was so strong, there was no separation between those two human beings, the rescuer and the rescued. That identification of common humanity was so compelling that he instinctively acted as he did.

One of the theories of evolution is that as we have evolved, acquiring more intelligence and brainpower, we have retained the residual need to try to save every member of our evolving human race. Each person is precious because they are part of our larger developing whole. Each beating heart, each pair of hands, each thinking brain is necessary to our collective survival. And it is this deep-seated need that emerges at a moment when life is at stake.

You even see it in cases that seem bizarre. At least four or five times, the award for bravery was given to somebody who was driving along and saw a person attempting suicide by throwing themselves into a river off a bridge. In one example, at the Fraser River in B.C., the driver leapt out of the car into the water, swam to a woman who had jumped off a bridge, and brought her to safety. In this case, the saving of a life mattered more than whether the woman herself wished to live. In all the cases in which this happened, I always asked the rescuer if he had ever had contact with the rescued person afterwards. In every case, he had not. A life was saved; a rescuer's life was risked. End of story. Perhaps it seems strange that there isn't gratitude, or that no Hollywood-style friendship or love affair ensues. Once that person is saved, life simply continues.

I believe that this is what happens to us when we see groups of people who are endangered. In 1951, which happened to be my first year in university, Canada took in fifty thousand Hungarians after the uprising against the communist regime. The University of Toronto, where I was a seventeen-year-old student, admitted an entire forestry school from one of the Hungarian universities. All of us at the time felt it was perfectly understandable that we should accept these people who came with nothing but were escaping with their lives. Perhaps I am more deeply marked by this because of my own childhood experience. There were other examples. After the war, we took in many refugees, and some had those tattooed numbers on the backs of their hands. We knew that we had to take them in. So when the Vietnamese boat people appeared in the headlines, it seemed inevitable that we should be part of this campaign to help. In the case of Operation Lifeline, the sponsorship groups were initially supported by the Conservative government, and the Liberal government carried it on: it was part of the government's plan to integrate the Vietnamese boat people into Canadian life, and as Fred Bild, our ambassador to Thailand at the time, says,

"We took in 150,000 eventually; they've all blended in." Operation Lifeline got a lot of credit from the media as being spontaneous and somehow self-managing. Actually, it was extremely well coordinated through government and other agencies helping people to organize local chapters.

Not all Canadians supported it. As always, on critical occasions like this, polls have indicated that Canadians are not supportive of large numbers of refugees coming into the country at any time, regardless of the reason. I've noticed that about seventy percent of Canadians have been against taking in a large group of, say, Somalis, Tamils, Vietnamese, whatever. And yet, on the ground and in reality, they accept them, even though the newcomers don't speak English and are of a culture that we don't understand or even appreciate. In Canada, we always seem to give much more than we say we are going to. There was a popular song when I was a little girl that went, "Your lips tell me no, no, but there's yes, yes in your eyes." That's the way we are as Canadians, lurching into doing the right thing. We're the opposite of so many other countries. We have a negative imbalance of good in us. Perhaps this is what's enabled us to take on all sorts of things that other countries couldn't possibly do. We know that other countries would not have admitted such a high number of Vietnamese refugees, and their reasons may have sounded rational, such as the refugees' inability to speak their language. These are concerns that have never, in the end, mattered in Canada, and this is what makes us different. We have been able to accept people on the grounds of our common humanity. Officially and unofficially, we have been able to say that we are all human beings and that no human being is less human than any other.

4

John Tran

In Hanoi, in the late 1970s, a little boy of six would carry cameras around his neck for his father. They would go off each day in a *tuk-tuk*, a three-wheeler bike with an engine, to a place called Sword Lake, and the father would lead the boy around as he took pictures of people. Then they'd go home and the father would develop the photos in a darkroom that he had set up in their little portable kitchen. The next day, father and son would return to Sword Lake to try to sell the photos to the people they'd seen the day before. The father loved to take photographs, but his main job was as a calligrapher for the Vietnamese army. He did beautiful calligraphy for calling cards for anyone wanting something special to show to people.

The little boy, Thang, whose name is now John, had an older brother, but it was John whom his father chose to take with him on his photographic excursions. Their tiny apartment was in an alley right behind a cinema. They could hear the soundtrack of movies being played in the theatre, and John remembers hearing a lot of

Russian voices. Vietnam had just become communist, and so the Russian influence was particularly strong.

John developed a passion for the movies—how people looked and moved in them, even when he couldn't understand the plots or the words. He saw how a face could fill a whole screen, and then how that screen could contain hundreds of people. Once, when there was a new film he wanted to see, he took his sister, Ann, who was about two years old. He was supposed to be looking after her at home, but he piggybacked her over to the cinema. She fell off his back and started screaming because her arm was hurt, but he told her not to make a fuss and they sat through the entire film. When he brought her home, they realized she had broken her arm and he was in big trouble. His father was very angry and hit him, but that wasn't unusual. Even though his parents loved him, his father often hit him.

John's mother was a nurse and worked mainly in clinics. His father did whatever was necessary to make money. The children were sometimes left in a temple where Buddhist nuns looked after them, or John would be put in charge of looking after his little sister or left alone with his older brother, Tim. But their situation was no different than that of many children. They were supposed to look after themselves. The parents were busy trying to make enough money to support them under the communist regime.

Although the Tran family was Vietnamese, like many of the boat people they were originally from southern China. Some of the boat people considered themselves to be more Chinese than Vietnamese, but it depended very much on the family and how long they had been in Vietnam. Nowadays, in Canada, if you go to Vietnamese stores you can hear both southern Chinese dialects and Vietnamese being spoken.

In late 1979, civil unrest was increasing and public demonstrations were becoming frequent, and the Tran family became worried about the future. John's father made a trip to see his brother in the city of Hai Phong, and the two brothers decided they wanted to leave Vietnam with their families. At that point, they thought they would be going to Japan. When John recalls that, it makes him laugh; he knows now that it was a fiction, a dream. The only contact John's father had there was a friend, and when he told his wife about his plan, she cried. She didn't want to go, but John's father was the boss. John's uncle, his father's older brother, ran a bike shop, and his father was doing all right as a calligrapher and a photographer, but he knew people were leaving in search of more opportunity. It was the idea of opportunity that appealed to him, the idea of doing something new, that was different, even though there was risk involved.

Although John's family had decent accommodation, there wasn't much money and food was rationed. John remembers that portions were very small and that they all saved some of their own food so that their little sister could get more. White rice was a rare luxury. They ate a lot of millet mixed with their rice and had fish and spinach. The ultimate luxury was condensed milk. When I hear people from countries like John's talk about condensed milk, it reminds me of Newfoundlanders I knew in the 1960s and 1970s who loved condensed milk so much they couldn't drink their instant coffee without it. But in John's case, condensed milk was a luxury because it was so hard to get.

John remembers that his mother cried and cried about leaving, but his father insisted they were going in three or four days. They would sell everything to the neighbours. To this day, John remembers the sounds of his mother sobbing. Before they went, his father made a bonfire in the centre of their courtyard and burned his negatives and photos. That image of the fire and the smoke and the pictures curling up has never left John.

Passage had to be bought on a boat, and a huge number of people wanted to get on those boats. Today, when I hear that people like the Trans have paid to get on a boat, I think, What else is new? If you had only one chance to leave, and you could pay for it, wouldn't you sell everything and make sure you spent every cent necessary to buy your passage? In my family's case, when we left Hong Kong it wasn't a matter of paying, but we had to present ourselves and hope that we'd be chosen. Somehow we were. I never found out from my parents whether they had brought any hidden valuables with them—American dollars, small pieces of jewellery— but they may have done. I will always remember my father telling me enigmatically never to buy jewellery as an investment because it could never be sold for much when you really needed the money.

The uncle in Hai Phong had bought tickets for the extended family, and it was then they learned that their destination was not Japan, but Hong Kong. But their hopes were still intact, and they felt they would eventually get to Japan from Hong Kong. John's father told the family that they would fly to Japan. He was probably making that up. This was all part of his grand plan, which the family accepted. It's always very interesting to see the shape people give to the narrative of their escape: there's one destination, and then it becomes another; there's no money, and then some has been scrounged from somewhere. It's all about improvisation, being nimble, and keeping your wits about you. It's also about watching and seizing the tiniest opportunity.

The Trans knew they were going to go on a boat, but didn't know what kind. They were expecting it to hold about one hundred people, but closer to three hundred were jammed into it so that the owners could make a bigger profit. They had some clothes with them, and John's father brought some of his cameras, and they'd stuffed away bits of jewellery and cash. They travelled along the coast of China because they had to stop to get fresh water the whole way. I remember seeing the vivid TV images of those boats lurching through the ocean and wondering what kind of hell those people were going through. Five-year-old John, his brother, Tim, and his little sister, Ann, were among those people. It was much better when they stopped, because they could get out and swim on the beaches. Sometimes there was a little town where they could go and visit small stores. The boat sailed alone; it was not part of a flotilla. One solitary boat in the huge ocean.

As always, John's father was resourceful. He thought that being a passenger with a bunch of cameras and three children wasn't going to make him special enough, so he told the people who ran the boat that he was a cook. And so he became a cook. He improvised, having never been a cook before. He figured he could do it as well as anyone. The perks included a small area that served as his quarters, into which he managed to jam his family of five. Unfortunately, John's mother and sister were very prone to seasickness. For John, it was an adventure, even with all the females in his family constantly vomiting.

The voyage from Hai Phong to Hong Kong took four weeks. There were many panic-filled moments. Once, the boat sprang a leak and they all had to help bail it out. The worst was the time when they met other boats—larger, better-equipped ones. They were boarded by some of the people on those boats, who claimed they were going to tow them to safety closer to shore. They passed around a large tub and said, "If we're going to help you, you have to contribute." So John's father threw in a camera, and other families put in a ring or a brooch—everybody had to give something. And then the bigger boat hooked a line to them and started towing them, but minutes later the thieves cut the rope and left them to drift: the terror they must have felt, robbed and adrift on the high seas. By a stroke of luck, they were rescued by a boat from the Hong Kong Coast Guard that towed them to shore in Hong Kong.

When they arrived in Hong Kong, they were immediately scooped up and taken to a refugee camp. John remembers waiting endlessly in line in front of desks where people took down names. To a little boy, it seemed like forever. As he filled out John's papers, his father changed his son's birth date to May 8, because eight is a lucky number for the Chinese. Maybe he thought it would bring better luck to them all. Maybe he thought it would bring the best luck to John. John has gone back to celebrating his birthday on May 2, even though all his paperwork says May 8. It's a mystery to John why *he* was given the lucky number, but he has always accepted it as just one of those things his father did.

The refugee camp was surrounded by barbed wire and was very overcrowded. I remember seeing the camps on the TV news at the time, as most Canadians did; perhaps that's when our compassion was stirred for these people who had been found on the sea and herded into these places. The quarters were even tighter than they had been on the boat, but the Tran family was hopeful that it would be safe and there'd be enough food. John's father immediately looked for something to do. John says he always had to be doing something; he could accurately be called a workaholic. He got a job immediately, working in the camp sewers. He got his children jobs, too, buying ice cream from people who were just outside the wire fence; they bought them for five cents each and sold them in the camp for a twenty percent markup. Right from the start, he taught his children how to work, and not only to work, but also to find work. He did this himself with a dogged and fearless determination. He put up with being in a sewer because it was a job, however filthy and smelly. His uncle, meanwhile, set up a little barbering business, because all he needed to do that were his hands and a pair of scissors.

They were there for seven months. John's brother, Tim, who was eleven, joined a gang that took advantage of the overcrowding and the inevitable anarchy of the camp to break whatever few rules existed. John feels that this was where his brother developed a mean streak and a taste for fighting, from which he didn't recover until he was converted to being a Jehovah's Witness in young adulthood in Alberta.

As time went on, John's father dropped the illusion that they were all going to Japan. They began to live a life that involved some measure of freedom: the city chaos of Hong Kong was an exciting revelation to all of them. They would sometimes be allowed out on a pass and ride in the funicular up the mountain in Hong Kong called the Peak. John remembers looking longingly in store windows and sometimes going to Jackie Chan kung fu movies. If there were any sexy scenes, his father covered the boys' eyes with his hands.

John's father suddenly announced that, instead of going to Japan, they were to go to Canada. Though they knew no one there and didn't speak the language, John, only six, didn't question it. The excitement was greater because it would be the first time he had ever boarded a plane. In January 1980, the Tran family arrived in Edmonton, Alberta. They saw snow for the first time. They were processed, put up in a motel, and given winter jackets, mitts, and scarves. John remembers very clearly his first sight of a Western toilet. There was a diagram showing that you were not to perch with your feet on the toilet seat in the way they had used latrines and outhouses in Vietnam, on the boat, and in the refugee camp. He learned quickly.

Different groups were sponsoring different Vietnamese families. His family and one of his uncles were linked to United Church groups in Calgary. His other uncle went to Mississauga, Ontario. John's family developed a warm and personal relationship with their sponsoring family; every Christmas and Thanksgiving, they celebrated together, and the Canadians became a special part of the Trans' family life. The two families are still very close, and the Trans call them grandparents. One of the sponsors was a doctor, and he became the Tran family doctor. The sponsors outfitted the Tran children with proper clothes for school and got them skates and taught them how to skate. Most important, they helped John's mother and father find work. Nobody in the Tran family spoke English, but their sponsors did their best to communicate through dictionaries, sign language, and occasionally finding someone who could translate. They muddled through, and even without formal lessons, English seemed to get learned. When the sponsors found out that John's father was a photographer, they found him work at a processing lab. Though he couldn't speak English, he knew everything about photography, so they knew he'd be able to press the right buttons. John's mother worked at an A&W restaurant as a dishwasher.

Because the parents were working all the time, John's older brother looked after him and his little sister. In the evenings, their parents tried to take some English lessons. The sponsors came every week to help them learn how to pay their utility bills and where to do their shopping. One of the sponsoring families owned a ranch, and it was exciting for the Trans to ride a horse for the first time. Their sponsor family also took them to movies like *Star Wars*. To John, *Star Wars* was a revelation; even though he didn't understand any of the words, the visual imagery, the fantasy, the thrilling arc of the story were things he has never forgotten. All that had begun in the alley cinema in Hanoi now bloomed in Edmonton's movie theatres.

The children were shown how to take the bus to their elementary school in the middle of the winter. John and Tim were the only Vietnamese pupils at their first school. John was entering Grade 3 and began classes in English as a second language. Then the Trans found another house in a low-income housing unit in the northeast of Calgary and switched the children to Catherine Nichols Gunn School. John's parents have lived in that working-class neighbourhood ever since. Huntington Hills became their neighbourhood, close to Deerfoot Mall.

It was about this time that the children decided to take English names. John's name had been Thang and his brother's Chin, and they became John and Timothy, chosen from the Bible by their sponsoring families. John was aware that their sponsors went to the United Church, but he doesn't remember ever being taken to church by them. In his own family, they still hung on to certain ceremonies in the Buddhist tradition—burning joss sticks and making offerings at little shrines to Buddha. Their sponsors made no attempt to interfere with any of this. They were, John says, extremely kind and encouraging and very proud of them when they visited.

Tim and John both had drawing skills, so when their sponsors came for tea, the boys would show them their drawings, which the sponsors loved to see. John learned to play hockey and played left wing. Tim was always a forward. But it was ball hockey rather than ice hockey, because as the years went on they couldn't afford the equipment. Tim was good with his hands and made hockey nets out of old hockey sticks and pads from old car seats. They played street hockey every day, even in the cold weather. These are John's greatest memories of growing up. Then they would go home, eat their mother's cooking, and do chores and homework. If it was a Saturday, they'd watch *Hockey Night in Canada*. It was the Gretzky glory years, the years of the Oilers and the Flames: two Vietnamese boys worshipped at the shrine of Number 99. When their sponsoring family occasionally took the boys to games, Tim and John were ecstatic. John has never forgotten the thrill of being in a hockey arena, seeing the ice and feeling the excitement of the crowd. But they had problems with his father. He refused to watch hockey because he considered it a waste of time, like all games. John always knew that his father had no idea what fun was; he thought anything that wasn't work was a waste of time.

In his art classes at school, John discovered he liked painting and doing murals. In high school, he became photo editor of the yearbook. By now, his father was doing photofinishing and haunting the pawnshops looking for old cameras. He dreamed of opening a vintage camera shop. He took John on these excursions to hunt for old cameras, teaching him what to look for. John learned how to clean the cameras and test them to see if they were working properly. His father took endless photos of the boys and their sister. In high school, John wanted very much to be part of things, so he joined a lot of clubs. Through his interest in the arts and in photography, he was able to be part of the football team even though he didn't play; he filmed the team and then edited the clips and added songs like "Eye of the Tiger" as background music. He would play the videos in the team's locker room to help motivate them. He says he wanted to belong, and photography and video helped him negotiate a place for himself between being a nerd and being one of the regular guys. In high school, he made friends with everybody, but his best friend stuck and later would become his best man.

Naturally, John's parents met other Vietnamese who were boat people, but his father didn't want to mix only with Vietnamese. He was very outgoing and liked his customers, and he wanted to move forward into a new society. He also knew that when he opened his vintage camera store, almost none of his clients would be Vietnamese. Although his English remained rudimentary, he was so fearless he would just forge ahead and speak his broken, ungrammatical version of the language, willing to laugh and make fun of himself. In John's documentary film about his father, you see the ever-smiling, ebullient little man radiating optimism and energy.

In Grade 12, John got a part-time job washing dishes at the A&W. One day, after he'd finished his shift, he was waiting at a bus stop on Centre Street at Sixteenth Avenue. He'd called his mother to ask if she could pick him up (they had a car by this time). He was sitting, wearing his headphones, when a car jumped the curb and hit him. He flew through the air and recalls putting up his arm to break the fall. The next thing he remembers is opening his eyes and feeling that his leg was broken in half. People rushed to him, and he remembers them saying, "Don't move!" He was taken to the Foothills Hospital, where they repaired his broken arm and leg. Later, he was told he'd been hit by a drunk driver, a woman.

The family was persuaded to sue, because the injury to his leg had been drastic. Complications set in, and they had to re-break and reset his leg more than once. The family won the suit, and the settlement money enabled John to go to Ryerson University in Toronto to study film. More important, nearly dying at such a young age changed his view of life. John knew then that he had to do what he really wanted to do. If it hadn't been for that almost-fatal accident, he might have bent to his father's will and drifted into helping at the camera store. He would have always been the little boy helping his father with his cameras.

After a year of physiotherapy and convalescence, John was ready to leave for Toronto. He had spent some of that year at a theatre in Calgary that showed art house films, watching movies by Kurosawa and Fellini and Truffaut. He was worried that his father wouldn't want him to go to Toronto, but once he told him about his dream and was accepted at Ryerson, his father's natural ambition kicked in and he was very helpful.

John's first year or two at Ryerson were very lonely. He was living downtown, but his aunt and uncle would often pick him up at a bus stop in the far west of Toronto and take him home for dinner. In his third year, he made new friends, with whom he still works in the film business. From the start, he knew he would succeed; he had self-confidence and passion, and he knew what he wanted to do. And he'd been involved with photography since he was five years old.

By his fourth year, John had shot eight short films. Unlike a lot of the other students, who thought they might direct or produce or edit, John never had any question that he wanted to be a cinema-tographer and use his eye. In his fourth year, he received the Kodak Apprenticeship Award, which provided funds to any company that would take him on as an apprentice cinematographer. He apprenticed with an Australian named Robert Draper, who came to Canada to do a movie. John worked on it with him, and from

Draper he learned about lighting and, like him, became a great fan of Fuji film stock and the images it can produce. He was learning his craft in the most basic way. The beginner cinematographer cleans the cameras, the lenses, changes film rolls. It's typically the work of an assistant, but at the start of their careers cinematographers perform these duties in order to know the equipment and what it can produce for them.

John began partnering with a classmate and started a film company called Moon Dog, which got commissions from Bravo TV and the Canadian Armed Forces, among others. He worked constantly, and eventually caught the attention of the prize-winning producer Kevin McMahon, which led to his big break, working on McMahon's film *McLuhan's Wake*. The film is a brilliant evocation of Marshall McLuhan, using visual language, which is non-linear and extremely powerful.

John then moved on to work on a film about Mozart for Rhombus Media. His work was good, and it was recognized by young, dynamic directors. It was obvious by now that he was going places. In the film business, starting young and working all the time is the way ahead. John was prepared to work twenty-hour days, every day, every week of the year. Commitment, ambition, and drive, in addition to talent, have given him his edge.

About this time, he met Siu, a Vietnamese production assistant working on a project he was involved in. Siu had also been born in Vietnam and was a refugee, but was not a boat person. She and her family had taken a mainland route out of the country and, like the Trans, ended up in a Hong Kong refugee camp. For him, it was love at first sight. He tried to sit next to her at lunchtime. For the first time, he asked for a girl's telephone number, and she gave it to him. But after a few months, she told him she really wasn't interested, and he was heartbroken. After a year, they ran into each other again, and she helped him get a job on a film she was working on. They began seeing each other once more, and one day, when they were sitting together at a table, he told her the person he loved was sitting right across from him. This time, she responded.

John was director of photography on the documentary *An Idea of Canada*, which Kevin McMahon made about my trip through the Canadian North as Governor-General. McMahon says, "John [would] hang through the open door of an airplane flying low over arctic tundra, braving -30-degree winds with a huge smile on his face, and come home with award-winning images." It was beautifully shot, and John was tireless as he trudged through the snow to set up his camera. And when we went across to Haida Gwaii, he caught the magical beauty of the rainforest and the Pacific coast, frequently wading through incoming tides to get the best shot. In 2010, he won the Canadian Society of Cinematographers Award for best cinematography in a documentary, Kevin McMahon's *Waterlife*. At the age of forty, he is one of the most sought-after cinematographers in Canada.

I went to Siu and John's wedding in 2004. It was held at a huge Chinese restaurant in Richmond Hill, north of Toronto. Some of the Trans' sponsoring family were there, plus a couple of hundred friends. It was a happy occasion. Looking at John, I wondered what he would have been had he stayed in Vietnam. When I asked him that, he said he certainly wouldn't have been a cinematographer; there wouldn't have been any opportunities. He believes he would have done just as his father did—hustling cameras, perhaps being a photographer. In terms of his cinematography, he feels that he's there for the long term with an art form that is still very young. It's barely a hundred years old. He thinks that with new digital and 3D technologies, he can always continue to develop his craft and open new ways of storytelling.

When John returned to Vietnam for the first time in 1993, he went to his old neighbourhood and saw that all the kids he had once hung out with were a foot and a half shorter than he was. They also already had children. At the time, he was in his second year at Ryerson. Looking in their eyes, he knew he could have been like them; he would have married young and had children, and would have had to make ends meet no matter what. By coming to Canada, his mother working as a dishwasher, his father working in a lab, his parents had done something for him that was no accident. They took their lives into their hands and risked everything for the future. It had made all the difference to him. Landing in Edmonton in the snow was the best thing that could ever have happened to the Tran family.

John and Siu made a documentary about John's father. Called *Daddy Tran* (John always refers to him that way), it reveals the man with all his idiosyncrasies, obsessions, and humour. They have taken their own history and made art of it. The little boy who came to Canada at age six has managed to incorporate into his own life the feeling that he will always be Vietnamese, will always love eating his rice with chopsticks. But every time he picks up his camera, John knows that great opportunity and joy are his because of the chance his parents took.

Carrying the cameras has brought all the pictures of his life into focus.

I DIDN'T BRING UP
MY SON
TO BE A CANADIAN

I Didn't Bring Up My Son to Be a Canadian was the title of a paper-back I saw when I was living in New York in 1968. It was the work of a parent seeking to protect their son from being drafted to fight in Vietnam. There were ways for young American men to avoid being drafted: attending college or graduate school, becoming a minister, getting married, having children, or declaring that you were a conscientious objector.

In Canada, certain members of the United Church took a stance and implored the government not to blindly follow American policy in Vietnam. They emphasized the importance of Canada as a place of political refuge. There is no question that Expo 67 and the celebration of our centennial had given Canadians new self-confidence, and it seemed to extend to politicians. Initially, when Pierre Trudeau made an official visit to Washington to see President Nixon and was interviewed by the press, he made an ambiguous statement to the effect that some servicemen from the United States were banned from Canada because of their legal obligations "at home." It seemed that Trudeau was trying to distance himself from a subject that, while in the back of everyone's mind, had not been broached by Nixon (though Trudeau did say that some deserters had already been accepted). But the stance of the Canadian government soon became more assured.

Former minister of immigration Jean Marchand declared during his time in Cabinet that he questioned whether there should be restrictions against U.S. deserters coming to Canada. Meanwhile, the United Church continued its strong campaign to accept the resisters (or dodgers, as they were commonly called) in and made the issue a test of the sovereignty of Canada. Controversy had raged in the pages of *The United Church Observer*, and one part of the membership wanted to help the resisters by offering shelter, financial assistance, and employment. Some of the membership also stated that they were "willing to administer to human need, of draft dodgers as of any other persons wherever needs exists." In 1968, the church's official newspaper observed that many United Church parishioners disapproved of helping draft dodgers, but on the whole the church's ministers approved. Directors of the United Church at the time wanted to attract young people and also to appear in the vanguard of new thinking. Some felt that the United Church wanted to show it understood current world affairs and to demonstrate its relevance. Other opinion makers and citizen groups felt that Canada could influence the American public's way of thinking about the war in Vietnam. With pressures on all sides mounting, Trudeau's Liberal government decided that draft resisters should be given fair treatment to emigrate to Canada, that they were resisting this particular war and weren't simply opposed to the principle of any military action.

Over a period of nearly three years, starting in 1969, Canada accepted more than fifty thousand draft-age Americans into the country. It was the largest group of Americans to emigrate to Canada since the arrival of the United Empire Loyalists after the American Revolution. In May 1968, Allan MacEachen, then the minister of immigration, announced the Cabinet's decision that all draft resisters and deserters from the United States would be given legal status in Canada as landed immigrants. With that stroke, any ambiguity about the status of those young Americans was clarified. Canada would not prosecute them, and they could take refuge under Canadian immigration law. As MacEachen stated in the House, "The question of an individual's membership or potential membership in the armed services of his own country is a matter to be settled between the individual and his government and is not a matter in which we should become involved." *The New York Times* trumpeted Canada's decision with the headline "Canada To Admit Any US Deserter."

It's pretty obvious from the way large numbers of resisters and deserters were accepted, officially and by the general population, that Canadians approved of the way our immigration laws reflected growing opposition in this country to the war in Vietnam. Like all Canadian ideas, it didn't go in a straight line starting from a firm belief and ending at a triumphant goal. Nothing in Canada happens that way. We tend to zigzag our way to a solution, but often it is the right one, even though getting there has been fraught with denial, compromise, and a certain obtuseness.

The United Church of Canada, the New Democratic Party, powerful members of the journalistic and academic elite, and, eventually, the government of the day—all for their own reasons— managed to persuade Canadians that American military service laws were irrelevant to Canada. And it was in this way that the American military resisters came to represent for us, as the writer John Hagan observes, "unexpected symbols of Canadian sovereignty." Not only did our unequivocal stance make a difference to the thousands of young men who came to Canada to escape the Vietnam War, but it changed us. It came to be a statement of who we are and how we behave as Canadians.

5

Andy Barrie

His voice has a tune in it that every listener can hum, but only he seems to know the notes. It's with this voice that Andy Barrie made a brilliant career for himself on radio in Canada, first in Montreal and then in Toronto. For many years, waking up for countless people meant hearing Andy's voice before you even heard "good morning" from the person you lived with.

As a young American army deserter crossing into Canada from the United States in December 1969, Andy was expecting something that resembled Checkpoint Charlie in the old Cold War days of Berlin. He thought there would be watchtowers, search-lights, and barbed wire. By the time he realized there wasn't any of that, he was already in Canada. He had come through Vermont and woken up a man in a little station at the Quebec border. The man gave him a friendly greeting and asked him, "Why are you coming to Canada?" Andy replied that he and his girlfriend, Mary, who was in the car with him, were going skiing. The official waved them on and wished them a good time. Andy still marvels at the way he got into Canada, but he felt it so strongly that he stopped the car, got out, and kissed the ground, because he didn't feel like a fugitive anymore. Now he thinks that might sound odd, but it doesn't sound odd to me.

My life in the 1960s centred around the University of Toronto and the CBC, where I started my career in television in 1965. Suddenly, at the end of that decade, there was an influx in Toronto of young men in their early twenties, all of whom were university graduates or undergraduates leaving their homes in the United States. And they were leaving for what they believed was a just cause: their opposition to American involvement in the Vietnam War. They were part of an American exodus and came to be known as draft dodgers. At first, it was a pejorative term, but it quickly became a more positive label. It covered the majority of young American men who refused to be drafted when they came of age. The laws stated that those who had been called to report were to be inducted into the armed forces. Those who applied to be conscientious objectors had to prove that they were pacifists or had religious beliefs prohibiting them from serving. Deserters were the most serious category, as they had been in the service and then left; therefore, the penalty of imprisonment was greater.

Andy was a deserter. When he and Mary crossed the border on December 23, 1969, they drove to the Queen Elizabeth Hotel in downtown Montreal and had a drink in Les Voyageurs bar to celebrate their arrival in Canada. Then Andy drove Mary to the airport so she could get home for Christmas. Her family was in shock; she had just informed her father, a retired admiral, that she was going to marry this Jewish disc jockey who was deserting from the U.S. Army. She had to go home that Christmas, but every year after, for as long as she and Andy lived in Montreal, they had a drink at the Queen Elizabeth on December 23.

Not only was Mary's father an admiral, but Andy's brother was a career military officer. Andy had been an undergraduate at Dartmouth College in New Hampshire. His older brother suggested that he join the Reserve Officers' Training Corps (ROTC) at Dartmouth because it would pay his tuition fees and assure an officer position if he eventually joined up. Andy did join the ROTC, but he was not impressed by his first contact with the military mind. He encountered men who he thought were martinets and who he believed had joined the ROTC in order to take advantage of positions of power.

When Andy entered Dartmouth in 1964, Vietnam was just becoming a controversial issue and people were beginning to question the participation of Americans in the war. Protesters then were still extremely well behaved; the men wore neckties to anti-war demonstrations. At one point, a serving general came to speak to them at Dartmouth. Naturally, nearly the whole school turned out to hear him, because it was a men's school and they would all be subject to the draft unless they had student deferments, stayed in university, or were conscientious objectors. Andy remembers very clearly that somebody stood up and said the Vietnam War was going to be a disaster and was immoral and evil. The general responded that when a football team elects a captain, they have to follow the captain's plays; that the country had a captain, their president, and they must follow his decision. He added that he knew things they didn't, and he believed they had to commit themselves to fighting the communists in Vietnam. Then somebody rose at the back of the room and said, "General, I would like to congratulate, in football terms, captains Goebbels, Hess, Himmler, and Hitler for over six million touchdowns." The whole place erupted into cheering and clapping. For Andy, that was an epiphany.

At Christmas 1966, he went home on holiday and applied for Conscientious Objector status. He began two years of hearings before he was given CO status, which meant he could be drafted as a conscientious objector and sent to Fort Sam Houston, Texas, where all medics were trained. He thought he would be shipped to Vietnam as a non-combatant medic, none of whom were given weapons training, but he applied for something called a Civilian Acquired Specialty, which was broadcasting. Obviously, other people had noticed what a terrific voice he had, and he felt he could use it in this way. Two years after graduating from Dartmouth he was drafted.

Andy was assigned to a unit that made videotapes to train medics. Voicing videotapes about wounds and sutures had its own element of craziness. But Andy had decided that if he got orders to go to Vietnam, he wouldn't go. He knew that too many medics were being wounded in Vietnam and that he would be called up soon. The war was escalating. When his orders came through, he went to his commanding officer and said, "I am going to desert, sir." He then asked if he could have his status at Fort Sam Houston made permanent because he had done such a good job, everyone said so, and he had got a commendation for creating new systems for scheduling videos. His commanding officer wished him good luck and told him he was sorry but he couldn't do anything for him. He also told him that he was not a deserter until a military court declared him to be. First, he'd have to go AWOL (absent without leave). Andy could tell him about his plan, but he couldn't get locked up for that. His commanding officer said, "I can't stop you."

Mary's father, the admiral, was also a pediatrics professor at Harvard, and at Andy's request he wrote a letter to the Surgeon General, who was a friend. Mary's father said that young Corporal

Barrie had done an exemplary job and asked if he might have his orders changed. Andy then actually went to see the Surgeon General of the United States, who agreed to meet him only as a courtesy to Mary's father. The Surgeon General told Andy he couldn't do anything now that he had received his orders; that would have been asking for special treatment. Then he wished him good luck. Next, there was a psychiatrist in New York who was willing to testify that Andy would lose his mind if he was sent to Vietnam. But Andy simply could not accept being called crazy; it was a question of pride. In fact, he considered himself extremely sane. Then he saw a lawyer in Boston who was going to find some way to get him sent to prison at Leavenworth and then intervene and get him out again. All of this activity happened within a month. But in the end Andy made up his mind to go to Canada, and Mary said she would go with him.

On the day that he was to be shipped to Vietnam, they drove across the border. Andy and Mary were prepared for the worst as they drove north in their little Volkswagen Karmann Ghia. Mary had come because she wanted to be with him, but also to provide the cover that they were going skiing. At that point, Andy didn't realize that Canadian Immigration people had been ordered not to ask anyone crossing the border about military service.

After bidding farewell to his *Mayflower*-descendant fiancée, he went to the Yellow Door coffee house on Aylmer Street in the student ghetto of Montreal. He had been told that if you were a deserter or a dodger, the people there would fix you up with a place to sleep. The next day, they asked if he wanted to have Christmas dinner with a Canadian family, and he said yes. I remember very well that in our circle of friends in the late 1960s, people were always circulating the names of the people who would like to spend

Christmas or Thanksgiving with a Canadian family; it was not unusual at the time. Andy's hosts turned out to be the family of Percy Talman, director of CBC English services for International Broadcasters (later Radio Canada International). He had landed right in the heart of broadcasting two days after arriving in Canada. Several days later, Talman introduced Andy to a senior executive at CBC Radio.

When he met her, she didn't have a job for him, but she told him about the biggest commercial station in Montreal, CJAD, and gave him Sidney Margolis's name. Having a direct introduction to the news director at CJAD didn't hurt, and when Andy turned up he was passed to the program director, Bill Handly, who would go on to be head of Standard Broadcasting. Andy later learned that Handly was an RCAF veteran who had trained pilots during the Second World War. Earlier, Andy had decided that in all good conscience he would immediately tell anyone he was asking for a job why he had come to Canada. He didn't want to avoid the issue and then be found out. Straightaway he told the general manager of CJAD, Mac McCurdy, that he was twenty-four years old, that he had worked a bit for Metromedia, a respected private broadcaster in the States, and that he had deserted from the U.S. Army. Andy fully expected to be kicked out the door onto St. Catherine Street, but McCurdy simply went on with the interview, making it crystal clear that interviewing a deserter from the U.S. Army was of no consequence to the general manager of CJAD. Mac then told him that he thought he sounded a bit American, so he asked him to do a demo tape. Andy had no idea what "American" sounded like, so he went back to his little nine-dollar-a-week room and listened constantly to the radio. He still has the notes he took— "been" and not "*bin*," "out" and not "*owt*"—which he has framed.

Four months later, he was deemed adequately Canadian-sounding, and amazingly to him he was hired to do the all-night show on weekends at CJAD.

Andy was proud of himself for finding a job. Although his parents were ideologically supportive of his objection to the war, they made no bones about the fact that they thought he was ruining his future. And although they were always on good terms with their son, they sent virtually no money, hoping that he would be starved into submission and come home. But Andy felt instantly that he was at home in Canada, that somehow there had always been a place in this country for him, that he had been, as he says, homesick for a place where he had never been.

Andy had another lucky break, which is also woven into the history of our rights and freedoms. He calls this part of his "creation myth." After being the all-night man for several months, he moved to a spot as one of the afternoon hosts. Four months later, in October 1970, the War Measures Act was declared and an announcer called Rod Dewar said on-air that he had gone to sleep in a free country and woken up in a police state. Summoned to Mac's office, Dewar was told that what he had done was seditious and that CJAD could lose its licence. Dewar himself, Mac continued, could be put in jail. The bottom line: he could not speak his mind on-air until further notice. Dewar then walked into the studio and swung the microphone, which was on a high boom, eight feet away from Andy while he was talking live. Dewar explained on-air that he was leaving and talked about the circumstances, ending his eighteen-year career in Montreal. And Andy got his job. There was an irony in the situation. Andy had come to Canada because he disagreed so profoundly with his homeland, only to find himself very shortly in the midst of perhaps the largest constitutional crisis we've ever had.

Andy never felt powerless in the way many people do who have escaped from their homeland. In fact, he felt empowered. By having made his decision to leave and having been a fugitive, he had suddenly become a useful and potentially important citizen. There were some ramifications for his family: his parents were visited by the FBI, who, interestingly enough, gave his parents Andy's address in Montreal (of course, they already had it) and told them they could go talk to him if they wanted. He never felt like a refugee. In those days, you could apply for landed immigrant status from within Canada, so he knew he'd be okay. He had a job; he knew how to write an English sentence. But he also felt he could be a janitor or sell gloves if he had to. He had confidence. And he was sure he wouldn't be what his parents predicted, a pariah forever. He'd been accepted by people who were not exactly counterculture types—general managers at private radio stations, people who worked at the CBC—which was a clear enough indication that they didn't think less of him because he'd deserted from the U.S. Army. People who had served in the Second World War and were executives thought he was fine and wanted to employ him.

Andy knew his parents wanted him to succeed. Their other son, who spent two years in Vietnam as a soldier, had fulfilled a lot of their ambitions even though he thought Vietnam was hell. At one point, Andy's father, who'd been a salesman and had visited Montreal as a young man, came up and took Andy to Ben's Restaurant, the famous delicatessen, which was a Montreal hangout for many years and had photographs of celebrities on every wall. They had a conversation in which Andy made it very clear that he didn't want to come home and have lawyers work on his case, that he was never coming home; he was going to stay in Canada. At that point, Andy's father called over the waiter and said, "This is my son, Andrew, and he's going to be a big radio star someday." And of course when Andy's eight-by-ten glossy photograph went up at Ben's, he told his parents, and indeed they were very proud of him.

Mary had joined Andy and they had married, but she never became a citizen. Her commitment was to him and to his life. Before Andy had got himself into the night job at CJAD, Mary got a job when she made a cold call to Sacred Heart girls' school. She had graduated from Sarah Lawrence with a superb education and come to Montreal where nobody had heard of Sarah Lawrence. Unlike him, she felt a stranger in a strange land. She went on to get a master's and a doctorate at the Ontario Institute for Studies in Education (OISE). And at one point years later, Dartmouth College head-hunted her, and she and Andy decided that if she was offered the job, he would follow her back to the States. That seemed to him to be the deal, but it didn't pan out. She continued to love her country even while becoming deeply involved with Toronto and its cultural life. It was she who developed the wonderful idea of the Cultural Access Pass to give new Canadians and their families free admission to the Art Gallery of Ontario for a year after they became citizens. That's how I got to know Mary, through the Institute for Canadian Citizenship, the foundation that is my legacy project from my time as Governor-General. The foundation acts to help new Canadians, from the moment they become citizens, to enter the mainstream of Canadian life. Mary created her program, which was adopted by cultural institutions all across the country, and there are now more than one thousand museums, science centres, and art galleries that follow this model. We owe it all to Mary Barrie. Mary died tragically too early of cancer in 2008 and did not live to see the huge success of her idea.

Like most Americans, Andy was brought up in a very patriotic atmosphere with the ideals of life, liberty, and the pursuit of happiness. The idea of American exceptionalism—that Americans had, in democracy, a particular and special gift to give to the world—was something Andy embraced, and as a teenager he was a pillar of teenage virtue. But he noticed in the early 1960s, and through a Cuban friend particularly, that the United States, which had been revolutionary, had repudiated the revolutionary dream. Particularly when President Batista was defeated in Cuba by Fidel Castro, he understood that perhaps his country had been on the wrong side of many world events. He gradually began to believe that in Latin America especially it had been on the side of oppression.

The idealism of his youth was gradually eroded by his realization that the United States had got into a very bad war in Vietnam. When Lyndon Johnson announced that he would not run for a second term, something was unleashed in him, and that was when he began to understand that he would not serve in that war. Just before he deserted, he went to see Second City, a comedy show in Chicago, and that night he heard a line he's never forgotten: "In order to enjoy the American dream, you've got to be asleep." He realized that Americans were asleep in a thousand different ways. He says, with complete lack of emotion, that the United States as a nation is psychotic, and by psychotic he means living in a reality that is not shared by others. He cannot believe what Americans will put up with, what they will swallow, what they believe. He says in a self-deprecating way that he has a phobic response to the United States, then he corrects himself and says he never really believed it was a phobia. A phobia is an irrational fear, and Andy believes that people have good reason to be fearful of the United States.

It was twelve years before Andy actually became a Canadian citizen, because he was constantly worried that his family might suffer or be harassed because of his being a deserter. But at some point he said to himself, "To hell with it," and became a Canadian.

President Gerald Ford declared a conditional amnesty for Vietnam War draft dodgers at the same time he granted a full pardon to disgraced former president Richard Nixon. As Andy sees it, Ford figured, "Nixon can be pardoned so I'll pardon draft dodgers." Not many went back at that time. When Jimmy Carter succeeded Ford as president in 1976, Andy's brother called him and said that AWOLs could return and be quietly discharged by the government. Andy called the American Friends Service Committee, the Quaker organization in Philadelphia, and they told him that it was legitimate. So Andy took a weekend off work at CJAD (it was about five years after he had arrived) and went to Fort Dix, New Jersey. They were all to be processed out there, and when he arrived they cut all his hair off, gave him new boots, and put him in uniform like the others. He was a little frightened at this point, because he was once again a creature of the U.S. Army. But he had the assurance of the Quakers that more than a thousand people had been processed this way. His barracks was filled with American men now living in Canada. He remembers somebody who was an apple grower in the Okanagan Valley and another who was a lawyer in Halifax. They were telling everybody that there was a Coke machine that didn't accept Canadian quarters. Andy arrived on a Friday, and on Saturday and Sunday they were marching and whistling "O Canada." They all enjoyed the fact that the kid who was marching them to the mess hall had no idea what they were whistling. On Sunday afternoon, Andy was officially processed out of the army on a general discharge. There is honourable discharge, general discharge, and dishonourable discharge. He was given a general discharge, and nobody in Canada ever asked him about it. Then he was given three weeks of back pay, his parents picked him up at the gate, and he went back to Montreal.

Many of the Americans who came to Canada agitated for amnesty immediately. Andy wasn't one of them. He believed he would never go back to the United States. He could vote as an American in U.S. elections, but he refuses. He says he won't rescue those people from themselves. He was told by many friends that he should have exercised his vote to help elect Barack Obama and defeat the Republicans after all he had seen done by the Bush administration, but he declined. He says if the Americans elect Republicans, then they deserve what they get.

He understands why some Americans in Canada stayed very American. They went on fighting the good fight as Americans. They were expatriates who were waiting for their Charles de Gaulle who would lead them back. Andy is quick to point out that there is no such term as American Canadian, equivalent to Chinese Canadian or Italian Canadian. He says there's no profit in calling yourself American Canadian. He's known people for years and didn't realize they were American—a city planner, a professor. People that he's interviewed—performers, lawyers, artists—just buried that part of themselves. He thinks it's a bit like being a transsexual, that you don't want to be reminded that you used to be a man now that you're a woman. It is, he says very seriously, like a gender change. Those parts he was born with were either cut off or they withered and died. He says that he feels he was a Canadian who grew up in an American's body.

Andy went on to become the most popular radio personality at CFRB in Toronto, where he was a respected liberal voice at a station not noted for its liberal views. He feels very strongly that he came at the right time to Canada, when Trudeau was making an impact on the country and was such an extraordinary contrast to President Nixon. Of course, the war was very unpopular, not only in Canada but around the world. The draft dodgers and deserters were the best-educated collection of immigrants that Canada has ever had. He realizes that admitting people like him into Canada was one way of "sticking it to the United States with virtually no cost," as he puts it, since the war was unpopular in the United States as well. It was just after Expo 67, which had strengthened Canadian pride, and the country felt it was on the cusp of something really magnificent. Many were disenchanted with the United States, and the contrast worked in favour of people like Andy. He felt that a lot of the broadcasters at CFRB were full of racism and homophobia and anti-Semitism, and he disliked Toronto when he arrived from Montreal. However, he continued to work there and became so popular that eventually he was lured to the CBC to do their morning program *Metro Morning*. He hosted that show for fifteen years. He retired in 2010, two and a half years after he told his listeners he had been diagnosed with Parkinson's disease. The disease takes its toll, but he has lost none of his punchy vigour. And he still has that voice that woke thousands of dreamers every day.

EXILES BY
MANY NAMES

When I first went to Nelson, B.C., in the late 1970s, I heard that this little city in the Kootenays had the greatest concentration of American draft dodgers of any place in Canada. I kept this in mind, and when I came to write this book I decided to make the trip to Nelson. When I was there I visited the nearby Slocan Valley. Its beauty is extraordinary, and I'd never realized that all those draft dodgers I'd heard about had come to an area where the Doukhobors settled after being displaced from their initial settlement in Saskatchewan at the beginning of the twentieth century.

Like many people who came in large numbers to open up the West, the Doukhobors were initially welcomed. In their native Russia, their beliefs were contrary to that of the established religion, the Russian Orthodox Church, and they had known only persecution. Many had been exiled to Siberia. In fact, in 2003, when I was in Russia on my state visit as Governor-General to the circumpolar countries, I asked to go to a former gulag near Salekhard. It was something I wanted to see with my own eyes—the place, dreary, vast, hopeless, that conjures up Solzhenitsyn's *One Day in the Life of Ivan Denisovich*. I wanted to compare it to our North. Indeed, it was similar to the Northwest Territories—boreal forest, broken only by the wooden remains of bunkhouses. We were taken to a place that had housed not only exiles from the communist regime but also Doukhobors and other persecuted enemies of the czar. We were told that it was from that very camp within the Arctic Circle that the Doukhobors had come to Canada.

The story is not known to many Canadians, or many Russians either. Leo Tolstoy, the great novelist, had been developing his own form of mystical Christianity, which emphasized a personal relationship to God without the intervention of organized or state religion. When he heard about the Doukhobors, he was very sympathetic to them and their beliefs. The Doukhobors were pacifists and wanted to live off the land and share their goods communally. Tolstoy sympathized with their spiritual beliefs and followed their communities' endeavours in Russia. They were always willing to work hard, and in fact that is one of the tenets of their faith: to work hard, to pray together, and to live a peaceful life. Tolstoy understood them. He knew about their persecution by czarist authorities and the imprisonment of their leadership in Siberia. Remarkably, he dedicated all the royalties of his last novel, *Resurrection*, to helping them emigrate to Canada to escape continued harassment.

Doukhobors refused to swear allegiance to any state authority. When 7,500 of them came to Canada in 1899, a deal was made with the minister of the interior, Clifford Sifton, that would exempt them from military service and allow them to enjoy freedom of religion and hold their land in common in the same manner as the Mennonites had done in coming to Canada several decades before. They settled in Saskatchewan on blocks of land totalling more than seven hundred thousand acres, where they established sixty-one villages. They not only farmed, but also constructed and operated brickworks, linseed oil presses, gristmills, and sawmills.

Sifton was replaced as minister of the interior in 1905. His successor, Frank Oliver, dreamed of a Canadian West populated by British immigrants and warned against the prairies, the "seat and cradle of the future population of this dominion," being filled by "people with different ideas ... different views" who would deflect Canada from the destiny for which he felt it was intended. He moved to cancel half of the homestead holdings of the Doukhobors because they would not swear allegiance to the Crown and would not take individual title to their land. This caused rifts in the Doukhobor community. Some refused to take the oath and were dispossessed, while others did take the oath in order to stay on their land.

In the turmoil that ensued after Oliver's edict, some five thousand Doukhobors moved in 1908, under the leadership of Peter Verigin, from Saskatchewan to the area around Castlegar, near the Slocan Valley in British Columbia. It was one of the largest internal migrations that Canada has ever seen. Here, they were able to take up land and were not required to take individual title to it; they became incorporated as a community, and as such could hold property. They accumulated nearly six thousand hectares of land, and within fifteen years Verigin had added another three thousand hectares to their property. They developed flour mills, a jam factory, sawmills, and electrical plants. Everything they earned (and some of them went to work on the railroad or as labourers for other farms) went into their communal coffers. Doukhobors believe that the land was made by God and belongs to him alone, and they were now able to live the life that they believed in.

The turmoil of relocation left scars on the community. But the move to Castlegar and the nearby community of Brilliant was something that they eventually accepted, and they began to create new enterprises in their new home.

⁓

The Slocan Valley nestles in a group of mountains known as the Kootenay Arc—a four-hundred-kilometre belt of Cambrian and Mesozoic sedimentary, volcanic, and metamorphic rock trending northeast for 160 kilometres across Washington State into British Columbia, then north along Kootenay Lake and northwest into the Revelstoke area. In these mountains, miners would find silver-lead-zinc ores called galena, and by the 1880s people were aware that this was an extremely rich mineral area. American entrepreneurs began coming northwards, having heard about valuable silver deposits. When one prospector found 150 ounces of silver per ton, the "silver rush" began, which lasted through the last decade of the nineteenth century. Within five years, more than three thousand claims were registered in Slocan, and the whole area boomed.

It was into this area that the Doukhobors moved in 1908 after they left Saskatchewan en masse. They hung on to their values against all odds, and have managed to sustain their beliefs even until now. Unfortunately, many older Canadians remember only the Sons of Freedom sect of the Doukhobors, who made headlines through the 1950s when they refused to allow their children to go to public schools. They regarded all government initiatives as an intrusion on their lives and in protest burned their own houses and the women took off their clothes. As a child, I remember seeing for the first time middle-aged women naked in photographs. I recall one image particularly, that of a large woman with white hair with three or four small children huddled at her knees and an RCMP officer looking studiously the other way towards a burning house.

The Doukhobors' actions were labelled "terrorist" at the time. But as sensational and self-harming as their actions were, there's no question that the Sons of Freedom believed what they were doing was right and that this was their only way of protesting. Their religious beliefs made them intransigent, however, and the police and the government reacted in kind. It is an unhappy story that shows that Canadians could not accept that the Doukhobors wanted to be left alone to live by their beliefs. They suffered massively from their confrontations with the Canadian authorities. Their school-age children were taken away from them and placed in residential schools, and the bitter memory of this still haunts them. The government also increased the penalty for indecent exposure (Sons of Freedom paraded naked in the hundreds) from six months to three years in jail. One child of that time, now an old woman, will never forget living on the side of the highway in a tent with her mother near the prison at Agassiz, where the men of their family were imprisoned for years for burning schools and their own houses.

The turmoil within the Doukhobors and the rift between the mainstream of the sect and the Sons of Freedom appear to have healed over. The events now seem remote in the beautiful peace of the Slocan Valley. The most important point of the Doukhobors' Christian beliefs is that they believe that God and Christ exist in every person and that God is manifested by what you do to other people. They reject the idea of ritual, liturgy, icons, and all the outward symbols that are very much part of the Russian Orthodox tradition. There is a kind of naïve belief that if everyone treats everyone else with compassion and kindness, everything will be all right. Hence their refusal to bear arms.

These are the people who welcomed American draft resisters to their area. I interviewed about half a dozen draft resisters and deserters, now in their sixties, in the Castlegar and Nelson area, and they all spoke highly of the Doukhobors. They recalled how helpful they had been to them in their early years, even those deserters who had been characterized in the press as marijuana-smoking, free-loving hippies. The Doukhobors helped them with their farms and shared their agricultural knowledge.

But this wasn't the only group that the Doukhobors helped. In his autobiography, *Metamorphosis*, David Suzuki recalls being befriended by Doukhobor farmers who gave help to his interned Japanese family—concrete help, in the form of fruits and vegetables. For it was in this same valley that the Japanese Canadians arrived after being exiled from the Pacific coast in 1942 by the Canadian government, who deemed them dangerous aliens who might all be part of a fifth column, or spies. In two days in January, the Japanese Canadians, many of whom had been born in Canada or had lived for two or three generations on the west coast, had been made to pack up whatever they could carry with them and to evacuate.

Bicycles, cameras, cars were all confiscated by the police. Thousands of their fishing boats were sold for a fraction of their worth, profiting white people who saw an opportunity and seized it. The houses of Japanese Canadians were sold also, and the proceeds were used to help defray the cost of housing them in internment camps. Japanese Canadians over sixteen were required to register with the RCMP and carry identification with them at all times. They were summoned to Vancouver's Hastings Park, held in livestock pens, and then forcibly loaded onto trains and taken to the interior. Eight thousand out of the twenty-two thousand evacuated from the coast were sent to the Slocan Valley. All of them, whether they had been born in Canada or their parents or grand-parents had been born in Canada, were registered as enemy aliens.

The Japanese Canadians arrived in the Slocan Valley in the winter of 1942–43. It was deep in snow, and the people arriving in New Denver and Slocan City were housed in tents. A group of houses was built on part of a ranch and was called the Orchard. Food was scarce that winter, but the Doukhobor farmers brought truckloads of produce to the interned Japanese Canadians. There was a tuberculosis sanatorium in New Denver for both the internees and local people, since TB remained a great scourge until the advent of antibiotics. A decade later, that sanatorium was used as a residential school when the children of the Sons of Freedom were forcibly taken away from their parents. The Canadian history wrapped up in that New Denver building is quite amazing: though it sits peacefully in an idyllic place, it was the site of much suffering by Japanese-Canadian TB patients and Doukhobor children.

With the arrival of large numbers of conscientious objectors, draft resisters, and deserters to the Slocan Valley in the 1970s, many of them highly educated, someone there joked that they had more Ph.D.s per square mile than the University of British Columbia. Some draft resisters came with a bit of money supplied by their parents in order to buy a property.

Perhaps it is a legacy of the Age of Aquarius that the draft resisters I meet now have stayed true to the beliefs they had forty years ago. I visited Gary Wright, a draft dodger who is now the mayor of New Denver. His home in the Orchard, originally built to house interned Japanese Canadians, is probably four hundred square feet in total, although its walls are substantial. When one of my friends lived in a similar house there during internment, it was packed with newspapers in the walls for insulation. These simple buildings look like winterized cottages now, and in the middle of the Orchard is a centre with a fine Japanese garden commemorating the internment period.

The resisters were, and most still are, environmentally conscious and on the left of the political spectrum. Another immigrant group of comparable size entering Canada was the wave of forty thousand war brides after the Second World War; but they came from every kind of background, and I'm certain that their voting patterns were just as varied as the rest of the general population. The draft resisters are something entirely different.

In the Slocan Valley, the merging of a number of cultures made for a very vigorous, thriving community. The intermingling of the Doukhobors with interned Japanese Canadians and American draft dodgers is one of those uniquely Canadian palimpsests—exceptionally dynamic and spiritually enriching.

6

Corky Evans

Corky Evans ran for the leadership of the New Democratic Party of British Columbia twice, placing second both times. He was elected in 1991 as an MLA and has been in and out of the legislature, holding Cabinet posts like Transportation and Agriculture. Unlike Andy Barrie, Corky Evans came to Canada after having been part of the violent demonstrations against the Vietnam War. He was always interested in politics as a teenager in Oakland, California, and felt politicized from the time he played President Lincoln in a school play about the emancipation of the slaves. He reassessed his early military aspirations after a conversation with one of his father's good friends who had been in the Second World War. Corky wanted to become an Air Force pilot. His father's friend responded, "Oh, that's a good idea, and then you can kill people from thirty thousand feet and you won't actually have to see it. You won't get dirty."

Young Corky heard the bitterness in that voice and it made him think twice about soldiering—even more so when his father's friend later committed suicide. By the time he graduated from high school, Corky had decided he wasn't going to serve in the Vietnam War. His father was a public defender, and he tried to discourage Corky and Corky's younger stepbrother, Andrew, from doing anything that might result in a prison sentence. Finally, he gave Corky his truck and said, "Take Andrew and go to Canada." They left, but somewhere in Oregon the truck broke down. At the same time, they heard on the news that Lyndon Johnson was not going to run for a second term as president. To them, it signalled the end of the war, so they turned around and headed home.

Corky was called up for the draft in 1968. It was a humiliating experience: at lunchtime, the sergeant marched them all across the street in their underwear to a stand where they ate hamburgers, and then marched them back to finish the physical. Corky locked himself in the men's room, kicked out the window, and ran. He didn't hide. He just wanted to carry on with his life. Surprisingly, no one followed up.

In October 1968, he agreed to go to an anti-war demonstration with Andrew at the local induction centre. Corky characterizes his stepbrother as a very gentle person, a vegetarian who wouldn't even use a leather belt because an animal had been killed to make it. Andrew said he wanted to gather with the pacifists, so they joined people who were committed to non-violence. They marched at 6 A.M. past all the bars and flophouses in Oakland with people spitting on them and calling them names. The non-violent protesters were supposed to sit in front of the induction centre's doors. Tens of thousands turned out for that demonstration, and it turned very ugly. There were thousands of cops armed with billy clubs, and Corky watched them beat people on the head. Luckily, he was able to use a garbage can as a shield, and then people started rolling cars over. It escalated into a huge riot. Meanwhile, when his stepbrother stopped to vomit after being exposed to tear gas, he was arrested for refusing to disperse. The police dragged him six blocks by his hair and put him in prison.

Corky hid from the police. Dawn was breaking, and African Americans were returning home from the graveyard shift at work. He watched as the police charged a woman carrying shopping bags and then beat her against a plate glass window; oranges rolled out of her bags. He remembers that detail clearly, and that when she fell, the cops picked her up and threw her over a garbage can and beat her again. He could hardly believe policemen were beating up an older black woman. But he says he was too scared to intervene. A young black man beside him hurled a garbage-can lid at the police, and when they turned around they saw Corky and chased him instead. He managed to get away.

Corky became involved in a few trials of people charged with offences surrounding that demonstration, and that was what made him decide to apply for the formal status of Conscientious Objector, which would be a legal way to avoid participating in the war. He went to Arizona to initiate that process and went to the Episcopalian (Anglican) church where he had grown up. His family had helped raise money to build the church. He asked the minister there to attend a hearing with him and testify that he was a Christian and a pacifist. The minister refused, and told him he was not welcome in the church and that he would be struck from the parish list. At his draft board hearing, Corky learned he would be inducted and sent to the war very soon.

By this time, Corky already had a partner and three children. They had heard that people in Vancouver were helping draft dodgers. So they headed towards the Washington–B.C. border. Corky did not have a university education, nor did his partner, Bonnie. They didn't have any money and they couldn't speak French. They weren't ideal immigrants. But people helped them and made arrangements for them to enter Canada. Corky got somebody to lend money to his brother, who put it into a bank account in Corky's name and mailed him the bank book so it looked like he had some money. There was also somebody on Vancouver Island who ran a place that hired illegal immigrants to keep the wages down, and Corky got him to write a letter saying that he would employ him. Then they drove to Seattle, got haircuts, bought some new clothes, coached the children on what to say, and came back to the border. They had been told that Blaine, Washington, was a tough border point, but when they got there they realized that the border officials knew what they were doing and they just let them in. Corky uses the word "miracle" to describe it. When they got to Canada, they were able to stay with friends in a logging bunkhouse with an outhouse and cold water, and they never looked back.

Back in the United States, his family imploded. His sister married a black man and was arrested—on false pretences, in Corky's opinion, because they had moved into a white neighbourhood. His father left the country and never came back.

Corky says they met hundreds of other people like themselves, that you couldn't drive down the road without seeing six young Americans hitchhiking. He went looking for jobs in the Northwest Territories, then to Victoria Island, and finally to the Kootenays. He did some firefighting at Kootenay Lake and saw a guy who had recently deserted who was still in his fatigues. He says the things that were happening then were "crazy." He found a community in the Kootenays, as so many other people were there for the same reason. He was stunned by the number of draft dodgers, deserters, and people who simply wanted to change their way of life.

He recounts that when his son Philip was born, they didn't have a doctor. He and Bonnie didn't have any money, and they didn't have a job between them. It was only about two months after arriving in B.C. It was midnight on Halloween, he was standing at the front desk at the hospital where Bonnie had gone into labour, and he was waiting for somebody to come and throw him out because he didn't have money. And then a woman came and said, "Your wife is upstairs having a baby. Don't you think you should go up?" He was stunned that he was in a country where you could have a baby before you paid.

Years later, Corky ignored the amnesty extended by President Carter in 1978. He had never considered returning to the United States. He felt it would imply that he'd only been in Canada because he didn't want to go to jail. People came to Canada, he believes, because they were looking for a country, and he found his. He is committed to it, and he has taken his place in mainstream political life with his unique fervour and commitment.

THE WORST PAIN
A MAN CAN SUFFER

In the mid-1980s, I accompanied John Ralston Saul to what was then Yugoslavia on several occasions: first to Ljubljana, the capital of Slovenia, and then to Zagreb. These were writerly occasions, with lots of wine and plum brandy (the lethal local variety called slivovitz). There were wonderful evenings of dancing in smoke-filled cellar bistros, with roasted meat, grilled fish, and shouted and slurred exchanges of English, French, and German. All the males I lurched around the dance floor with—teenagers with acne, white-haired poets with handlebar moustaches—told me I was so beautiful and must run away with them to the Dalmatian coast. The music, stringed instruments played with enthusiastic abandon, covered all awkwardness. The joie de vivre and excitement were wonderful, and we felt we were part of something marvellous. On the surface, the country seemed like ours: a federation of like-minded states where the similarities outweighed the differ-ences. We met Croatians, Serbians, Slovenians, and Montenegrins on that trip. Some of them murmured that perhaps disaster was approaching; but if anyone had told us that in a few years the whole thing would degenerate into a hideous war of ethnic and religious conflict, we would have said they were fantasizing a horror movie.

The breakdown happened as a result of the collapse of central communist authority in the late 1980s, soon after our visits. Nationalists in each republic, who until then had been very marginal, moved into the mainstream. What had seemed extreme became the norm almost overnight.

Yugoslavia began to rupture along a multitude of religious and ethnic lines. As chaos descended, Serbia, the most powerful of the six republics, attempted to assert its dominance; Croatia and Slovenia's nationalist movements were alienated, and subsequently Bosnia's. They all declared independence in 1991. But of course there were problems: ethnic Serbs in both Croatia and Bosnia resisted their new governments' call to rally around bloodlines. The situation degenerated into several distinct civil wars within the new republics.

It was difficult for Canadians to understand exactly what was happening. Back then, I was like any other reasonably informed Canadian, feeling sad and helpless while a formerly civilized country swiftly broke down into savage segments, their citizens tearing at each other's throats. Canadians, as part of the United Nations Protection Force, donned their blue berets to help bring peace to the former Yugoslavia. We were accustomed to acting as peacekeepers; Canada, under Lester Pearson's leadership, had developed and refined the role since its beginnings during the Suez crisis of the 1950s. But it was in the former Yugoslavia that we came up against the brutal reality that we were no longer helping to keep peace but had become engaged as combatants.

The Medak Pocket incident was carefully explained to me when I became Governor-General and Commander-in-Chief of the Canadian Forces in 1999. Early in 2001, I was to present the Commander-in-Chief's special commendation to the Princess Patricia's Canadian Light Infantry. The 2nd Battalion of the PPCLI was being recognized publicly for performing a military deed of "a rare high standard in extremely hazardous circumstances"—in other words, a deed that brought great honour to Canada and benefited the reputation of the Canadian Forces. It continues to stand today as a moment of dramatic courage.

In 1993, Croatian forces had attacked the village of Medak ("the pocket") and expelled rebel Serb forces. Between September 9 and 17, the fighting was criticized internationally, and the Croatians, under pressure, agreed to a ceasefire and a withdrawal to the start lines of September 9 negotiated by the UN force commander, the French lieutenant-general Jean Cot. Charged with overseeing the withdrawal and protecting local civilians were Lieutenant-Colonel James Calvin and 875 troops of the Princess Patricia's 2nd Battalion. The Patricia's were not only made up of highly skilled regular soldiers and technical trade groups, but were heavy on reservists who were volunteers from militia units across the country. The troops were instructed to place themselves between the two warring factions while the ceasefire was implemented. Suddenly, they were in a war zone, fending off a Croatian infantry brigade equipped with armour, mortars, and artillery.

Between the time of the negotiation for the ceasefire and the withdrawal of the Croatian forces the next day, the 2nd Battalion watched helplessly as the Croats engaged in a last crazed frenzy of "ethnic cleansing" against Serbs, killing men, women, children, and even Serbian livestock as they withdrew to the negotiated line. We cannot imagine what the 2nd Battalion, as military men trained to use disciplined force, must have gone through. The great historian Herodotus said, "This is the worst pain a man can suffer; to have insight into much and power over nothing." The Princess Patricia's performed armed and determined peacekeeping, defying intimidation and direct fire. It is not what we have in mind when we think of keeping the peace and patrolling carefully controlled neutral territory. They witnessed and helped to document Croatian war crimes, but they were helpless to stop them. Our soldiers did everything possible to keep the peace, but the problem was so huge they could not be totally responsible for making the Croatians cease and desist. In the overall war situation, the Serbs were not blameless either. There would be many other massacres, and larger ones, before the necessary political will was summoned up to help to stop the ethnic cleansing.

The commendation was coming eight years after the action, as a result of bureaucratic hesitancy and governmental embarrassment about the status of the Armed Forces after the disgrace of Somalia—events completely unrelated to the situation in the Balkans. The military who had behaved so valiantly at Medak Pocket were, I believe, intentionally not rewarded for their heroic actions because the Canadian government simply didn't want to hear anything about any of our Armed Forces. I became determined to do everything I could as Commander-in-Chief to re-burnish the reputation of the people who had willingly entered our military to do the right thing under the direction of our government. Even though I gave that commendation to the entire 2nd Battalion, there were many who couldn't attend the ceremony because they still suffered from the effects of post-traumatic stress disorder. I asked senior people in the PPCLI and my staff to organize private meetings in Winnipeg before the ceremony with a number of soldiers who had indicated that they would not come. We had a meeting of a couple of hours together, and I heard them describe, with great honesty and pain, their part in the action and how it left them crippled in many aspects of their lives. It made me realize what kind of sacrifice we ask of our troops, and how unprepared we are in peacetime to prepare others to deal with war. Medak Pocket and the engagement of Canadians in that incident will mark us forever. My relationship with the Patricia's will continue for the rest of my life, as I was honoured to become their Colonel-in-Chief in 2007, the first Canadian to hold this position with a Canadian regiment. I know I will not be the last.

Medak Pocket made us realize that keeping peace is not simple. Peacekeepers not only hold the battle line: they *are* the battle line. The peacekeeper takes it from both sides. Today's peacekeeping, such as we have known it in the former Yugoslavia and today in Afghanistan, involves armed struggle. As Virgil said, "These shall be your skills: to impose ordered ways upon a state of peace, to spare those who have submitted, and to subdue the arrogant." I think our Canadians lived up to that task in a way that all who understand the difficulties and compromises and grey areas in this world must recognize: that you must resolve conflict peaceably if you can, but forcibly if you must.

By the time I arrived in Bosnia on a visit as Commander-in-Chief in 2001, the Dayton Peace Accord, brokered by U.S. diplomat Richard Holbrooke, had been implemented. Canadians were holding down several sites that were being manned mainly by the Royal 22nd Regiment of Quebec. We visited Drvar and Zgon, both of which encampments were installed in former industrial buildings, in the case of one a bread factory, in the other a carpet factory.

There was peace, but it had come at a terrible price. As Governor-General, I went to Sarajevo and met with people who had suffered through the war—newspaper editors who had lost journalists, and others who had lost relatives. The strangeness of people having to declare themselves as Serbs or Croats made an absurdity of what that federated nation had been. I couldn't help but think that if Canadians had to start declaring what parts of us were of what ethnic origin, our country might collapse into a kind of dark comedy. In one particularly moving case, a Jew from Mostar said there was no longer a place for him: he was Serb on one side, Croat on another, yet wholly Jewish, but Jews were not an ethnic category under the Dayton Peace Accord. The Sarajevo I saw was a battered place; the last really shining memory of it, from the 1984 Winter Olympics—when Sarajevo welcomed the world to the life-enhancing and peaceful celebration of worldwide sport—was rubbed out. This is a lesson that we should not forget.

To become a citizen of Canada and commit to its democratic and egalitarian ideals, you are not asked to erase your memory. You may come with whatever baggage you wish to bring. Canada is not like the French Foreign Legion, where, when you join, nobody asks you any questions and nobody has a last name. This is the enormous benefit of a country like ours, where choice is possible, but you don't have to make every possible choice. We do not demand that anyone fit a certain pattern, and this gives us an ease with ourselves and with others. It gives us true liberty, the freedom to be what we want to be while adhering to the rule of law and the customs of the country.

Thoughts like this put me in mind of the Serbian writer David Albahari. I had been following David's literary progress in small magazines like *Geist* in British Columbia, and was fascinated to learn he'd been writing in Serbian in Calgary since 1992. When I heard that he was considered one of the great Serbian writers, I was even more intrigued. My old instincts as a television producer came out; I thought how great it would have been if I'd done a program on him for *Adrienne Clarkson Presents*! It's not often I have those reflexes anymore, but I certainly did when I learned more about Albahari.

It wasn't the first time that Canada had housed a great writer who contributed to the literary culture of another country. Stefán G. Stefansson, the genius of Icelandic literature, lived in Markerville, Alberta. Icelanders (who, with one hundred percent literacy for at least a century, are the most literate people in the world) were enormously influenced by Stefansson's writings. Although he lived practically all his life in Canada, he was considered a true Icelandic nationalist, and from his home in the Prairies understood the place of literature in history.

Basically, he was a farmer, raising cattle and sheep, and was the first member of the Icelandic settlement in Markerville to harvest rye. He worked in a local creamery, was a justice of the peace, and a member of the local school board. I suspect he is not more celebrated in Canada because he marked himself as violently anti-war during the First World War:

> In Europe's reeking slaughter-pen
> They minced the flesh of murdered men,
> While swinish merchants, snout in trough,
> Drink all the bloody profits off!

Stefansson was always honoured in Iceland and still is considered to be one of their greatest modern poets.

Having some knowledge of the Balkan situation, I was excited to acquaint myself with the work of David Albahari. Canada has always provided a place for people of great artistic talent, whether native-born or not, to express themselves. We have the space, the physical beauty, and the sense of leaving each other alone that greatly helps any kind of creative activity. Also, as David is Jewish, I was interested in finding out how the ethnically based conflict in the former Yugoslavia had affected him personally. He is one of the few people in this book I hadn't actually met before I started to research and write it, but getting to know him has been enormously rewarding. The fact that he has lived for nearly twenty years in Calgary, and is very connected to diverse young writers from East Indian and Portuguese backgrounds, as well as to native-born Canadians and the older writer friends who brought him to this country, says a great deal about our ability to accept and give space to people who have developed their talents elsewhere. It is part of how we offer the scope within our own psyches that comes from the enormous country we live in; it translates into the freedom we can provide other people as they come to join us here. There is room for all of us.

7
David Albahari

For Canadians, watching what happened in the Balkans at the beginning of the 1990s was horrifying. To see a federation break up—Yugoslavia comprised Croatia, Serbia, Slovenia, Bosnia, and Montenegro—made many Canadians feel nervous, because our own country is also a federation. But for those of us who had visited Yugoslavia and had Yugoslavian friends—who were of Serb, Croat, or Montenegrin origin—it was heart-wrenching. There was no way to explain it in a coherent fashion, and, most tragic of all, history seemed to be repeating itself in this ugly manifestation of civic breakdown and resurgence of ethnic hatred.

The writer David Albahari, already a well-known Serbian novelist at the time, was in the middle of this. He was in his forties, living in Belgrade, and, like many writers who grew up during the Cold War, was extremely well connected not only to his own writing community but to writers in other parts of the Soviet bloc. Yugoslavia, perhaps because of the singular leadership of Marshal Tito, enjoyed more freedom than many other parts of the Soviet empire. In the 1970s and 1980s, it was not unusual for Yugoslavs to travel abroad and attend conferences, whereas East Germans, for instance, could not. There was something about Tito's Yugoslavia that made it like the mouth of a shell rather than the hard wall of the shell itself.

David grew up in this atmosphere, travelling a bit when he was younger to different parts of Europe. After watching his own country break up, he arrived in Canada in 1992 and was just getting adjusted when the 1995 referendum over Quebec separation took place. He watched it with a kind of shocked recognition. As the numbers for "yes" and "no" to separation seesawed between forty-nine and fifty-one percent, he asked his wife, "Can this be real?" They couldn't believe that what had just occurred in Yugoslavia might also happen in their country of refuge.

David was very familiar with the process of a country's breakup and its potentially violent outcome. When Croatia declared its independence from Yugoslavia, the Serb population in Croatia declared that it would stay with Serbia. The acrimony turned into a civil war. David and his wife were reassured by their Canadian friends that nothing like that could happen here. David was skeptical. As a Serbian, he felt he understood more deeply, while on some level not understanding at all, what was going on in Canada. When Aboriginal people from Quebec announced that if Quebec separated they would stay with Canada, David likened it to the statement the Serbs made in Croatia. He became even more apprehensive.

Talking to him, I could understand why he felt nervous; the arguments for separation were identical. We, however, have not been attached for many centuries to a particular territory in the way the Europeans have. Territory equals nationality equals language, and in the small geographic area of the former Yugoslavia that has made for a tenacity and a fierceness about belonging that doesn't prevail in Canada to the same degree. Space gives people a chance to reflect, and when we think of the enormous territory of Quebec alone, as well as the gigantic reality of Canada, the second-largest country in the world, it's hard not to believe that compression into a small space exacerbates difference and renders compromise difficult.

David felt this very strongly coming out of the terrible conflict of the Balkans. In his novel *Globetrotter*, set in Banff, Alberta, his Canadian hero has a vision of a civil war in Canada. In the novel, the Canadian is influenced very much by a Serbian writer who seems to poison him with stories about negative nationalism. This novel has been translated into French but not yet into English. All of Albahari's novels are published by the prestigious French publishing house Gallimard, but the handful of his books published in English do not give us total access to him as a writer. If all his novels—there have been eleven so far, and a number of collections of short stories—were translated into English, we would recognize his tremendous talent.

Quite simply, he is considered by many to be the greatest living Serbian writer. There is one novel in particular, *Götz and Meyer*, that is widely thought of as a masterpiece. Published in 2004, *Götz and Meyer* is a short, devastating book, filled with black humour, and it is the most moving inquiry into the evil of the Holocaust that is possible to imagine. Two SS soldiers, Götz and Meyer, who together are responsible for killing seven thousand Jews in the Belgrade area, are dissected in the novel with a penetrating imagination that takes nothing away from the horror of their deeds and the empathy we feel for the victims of this relentless, meaningless tragedy. Götz and Meyer drive a truck taking Jews from a transit camp to Belgrade; the vehicle is a gas chamber of carbon monoxide, its fumes slowly killing its human cargo. It is one of those books, impossible to put down, that transforms your idea of what human beings are capable of doing. With unnerving clarity, David describes the interior lives of two people who represent all the evil humankind can enact. And yet through all of this, there is a thread of humanity that makes us understand how these acts were committed. His prose, exquisitely translated, has a light, almost ethereal, quality and plays in your mind against the horror of the situation being described.

David feels he was able to write this book because he came to Canada and maintained a healthy distance from his country of origin and his identity as a Serbian. He researched from afar the actual extermination of the Jews in Belgrade. Had he not been living in Canada, he feels he couldn't have reached so deeply into the past to seek out the real facts and real witnesses' accounts from which he created his story. Götz and Meyer were real people, and the novel is constructed around their historic and awful deeds.

Like many people, I've read a lot about the Holocaust, but this book had the deepest effect on me, probably because it brings together that very elusive thing that we can only call truth—the reality of those two men's lives and the documentation of their actions combined with the imaginative reconstruction of how they performed their ghastly mission in businesslike fashion day after day after day. These two men, actual SS soldiers, are, as Albahari says, the best proof of how technology allowed a trait to flourish that was inherent in the human personality. The horrible efficiency of the method of killing Jews puts into stark relief all our questions and assumptions about what it is to be truly human. Or, as the novel's narrator says,

Life is full of tricks, anyway, in war and in peace, it makes
no difference. It is always that same convulsive effort to
survive just a little longer than planned. Present or absent,
God is cruel, there is no genuine mercy in him. When he
blinks, he blinks and there is absolutely nothing to be done
about it. Souls cluster around him, voices waft his way like
the sound of a thousand little bells, but God merely shrugs
them off. ... Some things are simply stronger than all the
human spirit creates.

This acknowledgment of evil is all the more forceful because of
David's deliberately spare style.

There are autobiographical elements in *Götz and Meyer*. David's
mother's first husband and one of her children were killed in the
Holocaust, as well as his father's first wife. David's parents met after
the war, married, and started a new family out of the ashes of what
the Nazis sought to annihilate. The narrator says, "We'll be sorry ...
if we ever stop telling stories because, if we do, there will be nothing
to help us sustain the pressure of reality, to ease the burden of life on
our shoulders ... life is the absence of story."

Here is the essence of what David writes about: the novelist
must tell the story, because life, with its chaotic patterns, doesn't. In
the way in which David has chosen to live his life, he is creating his
own narrative, as we all do. And in giving his novel a narrator who is
an alter ego based on himself and his destroyed relatives, he manages
to create a reality that makes bearable that which is unbearable.

Émigrés and refugees are able to examine their native countries
and their contradictions, their traumas, their bitterness, because
a different knowledge comes out of loss. Those of us who have
suffered loss—in a war, or in any kind of upheaval—have been
forced to come to terms with the reality of what it is to lose.

In David's case, he has been fortunate in being able to go back and forth to Belgrade. He is celebrated as a Serbian writer and feels happy his work is appreciated. But he finds peace to write only in his basement in Calgary, especially in the four months of winter. When he travels to international book fairs, festivals, or to his original home in Belgrade, he is distracted by phone calls, demands on his time, and the insistence of people wanting him to be involved in various causes. Canada has given him peace, quiet, and detachment of the best kind. This detachment without alienation is one of the most rewarding things Canada can offer to those who have come here from rich, fulfilling (even though often disturbing and traumatic) backgrounds. Canada offers a kind of equilibrium in which, if you are a creative person, you can find your way. Fellow writers like Myrna Kostash and Ken McGoogan are very admiring of David Albahari and have given him great support in Alberta. But there are many more people who know him only as a sixty-year-old man with an accent. This benevolent bestowing of anonymity is something Canada does well, and it has benefited many. It's a kind of negative capability that can foster great creativity.

David was very involved with the Jewish communities in Belgrade when the war in Bosnia began. Members of the Jewish community of Sarajevo decided to leave in 1992 before the real fighting began. David was then president of the Federation of Jewish Communities in Yugoslavia, based in Belgrade. He was in charge of the operation to transport several hundred Bosnian Jews to safety in Belgrade. The Jewish community in Belgrade numbered only about fifteen hundred people, but he had support from Jewish communities in Europe and the United States who were concerned about events in Bosnia. At the time, he, like many others, thought the civil unrest would last just for a few days; an army plane brought people in from Sarajevo with just one small bag each. It was only after the days stretched into months that they all realized the position they were in. The federation began asking Jewish communities all over the world to take in Bosnian refugees. David made contact with the Canadian embassy and was then asked if he would like to join the group that was leaving for Canada. He declined. But by 1994, he realized that things were getting worse, and would continue to get worse, so he wrote to the noted Edmonton writer Myrna Kostash, whom he had met through literary circles, and asked if she could find him a place to escape to for a couple of weeks—a way for him to get out of hell for a bit. He felt he was losing his ability to work as a writer; all his energy, all his thoughts, were engaged in helping other people leave. He realized with a jolt that if he kept doing what he was doing, he would be finished as a writer. Myrna Kostash involved Alberto Manguel, who headed the arts journalism program at the Banff Centre, and Manguel invited Albahari to give a couple of lectures at Banff.

Albahari woke up on his first morning in the Rockies and saw spectacular mountains and endless trees. It was a startling contrast to what he'd been living through for the last three years: guns and bomber planes a hundred kilometres from Belgrade and the ceaseless effort to relocate others to safety. Though he was supposed to be in Banff for only a few weeks, a wonderful opportunity presented itself for him to be a resident non-Canadian author for one year at the University of Calgary. The person who had been chosen was suddenly unavailable, and David could replace him. He dressed up and put on a tie for his interview, only to learn that it would take place at a barbecue. He felt he had rather overdressed for the occasion. What really sold him, besides the beauty of Banff and the warmth of the friends he had already made in Canada, was the fact that the fellowship at the University of Calgary allowed him to bring his entire family for the year. His son was eight at the time and his daughter was three. It was a magnificent opportunity, but he still worried. "What will I do as a Serbian writer in Canada?" he thought. "What will my wife, who teaches English to Serbians, do? We're coming to a country where nobody reads Serbian and everybody speaks English." After eighteen years, he's still quite amazed that he came here and continued to write in Serbian, and his wife, as a trained teacher of English, got a good job teaching English to new immigrants.

David has been a Canadian citizen for more than ten years, and he realizes that this has come to mean a great deal to him. His eyes were opened in Germany when people kept talking to him about Canada. He asked them why they, living in one of the richest countries in Europe, should be so obsessed with Canada. They would tell him it was the space, the natural environment, the feeling of being able to expand that appealed to them. He struggles with the idea of what it means to have become a Canadian, and refers to the writer Joseph Brodsky, who himself was an exile and an immigrant to the United States. He points out that exile and immigration is a linguistic event. So much that happens is about the language of communication, and the language in which you choose to write, and the language in which you must live. David continues to write in Serbian but says he thinks more and more in a Canadian way. He doesn't think in English; his mind has developed a Canadian perspective that he uses as a kind of tool, sometimes a defensive one, whenever he might need to explain a position. When talking to him, I sense a certain linguistic apprehension initially, perhaps because he is an exiled novelist, living in a world that communicates in a different tongue, who writes in a language that seems totally private and aimed across a continent and an ocean. His career and profile are increasingly dependent, as the years go by, on the translation of his works into eighteen or twenty languages, none of which he can read. And then there is the diluting influence of Canadian society, culture, and customs.

∽

David Albahari admits that his first impressions were stereotypical—that Canadians were so polite you never really knew what was going on behind the niceness. When he first came to Canada, he wrote articles for Serbian newspapers in which he described the politeness and the unemotional quality of Canadians. In his novel *Bait*, he uses these stereotypes because he needed to explain to a Serbian audience what they were before he demonstrated that they were false. In the course of the novel, he shows that the coldness, the lack of emotion, is not really accurate.

He evolved as a writer when he realized he should be writing differently now that he was in Canada. His initial love was the short story form, but gradually he came to realize that he couldn't write short stories anymore, because they always took place in Belgrade, and he was no longer in Belgrade; he was in Calgary. He recognized how strange it was to be sitting in the basement of his house in Calgary, in minus-twenty-five-degree weather, thinking about and writing about Belgrade, where it's never that cold. It caused him to change perspective. Still, even if his perspective has changed, his internal language is Serbian. The substance of his writing will not change, but some of the settings are now in Calgary, in Canada.

Talking to David at any length about writing is very exciting. You get the sense that he is really plumbing the depths of what it means to express himself as a writer. It's not quite the same thing as Joseph Conrad, the native Polish speaker who became one of the great masters of English prose, or Canada's Nancy Houston, who has chosen French over English as her vehicle for literature. David's writing in Serbian is an expression of the total Serbian culture from which he comes. When he writes an article in English for *Geist* magazine, he writes things that he wouldn't write in Serbian. They are non-fiction and experimental, and while he enjoys doing it, it is completely different from anything he would think of doing in Serbian.

David is Serbian but he is also Jewish, and he points out that the war in Yugoslavia was perhaps the only example of a European ethnic war where Jews were not selected as a target. In all the other wars, Jews were made scapegoats. During the breakup of Yugoslavia, the Jewish communities of whatever linguistic background—Serb, Croat, Montenegrin—all wanted to stay together as long as possible. There were about seven thousand Jews in the former Yugoslavia, a relatively small number. Amazingly, many Yugoslavians suddenly wanted to reveal themselves as Jewish, citing their mothers or grand-mothers. They were explicitly shunning the ethnic identification as Serb, Croat, or Muslim. It was, ironically, one of the few times in history when Jews felt safer identifying themselves as Jews than as members of any other ethnic group. They had come from mixed marriages and had complex identities, but suddenly it was the Jewish identity that seemed to be helping people get out unharmed from a terrible war. David, as president of the Federation of Jewish Communities in Yugoslavia, had thousands of people coming to him with documents that proved they were Jewish.

Albahari is a Sephardic name, and David grew up as a secular Jew. His mother had converted to Judaism to marry her first husband, who perished in the Holocaust, and her second husband, David's father, was also a Jew. His father was deeply religious and went to a synagogue in Belgrade, yet David himself did not have a bar mitzvah. His family did celebrate the Jewish holidays at home, and he definitely feels that culturally he is a Jew.

David has found that in Canada the Jewish community functions in a different way, with a more religious perspective. He feels he would have to join a synagogue to be accepted fully into Jewish society here. Because he grew up in a secular society with many mixed marriages, he does not feel that he fits the definition of what Jews are in North America. He found that the way in which Jewish society was organized here was simply very different, and he has come to accept that the huge diversity of Canadian culture makes the Jewish culture only one of so many.

He came up against another cultural difference when he was asked to do some book reviewing. He found he didn't understand the way books were reviewed in Canada. Here, reviewers are expected to summarize the book's contents as well as critique it. In Serbia, it was almost a rule that you never wrote about what was actually in the book. You would criticize the style, or discuss the value of the message, but you would never retell the story. What is, or seems to be, valuable in intellectual terms is also different in Canada. That the same number of column inches in a newspaper would be devoted to a crime novel by James Patterson as to the latest José Saramago novel is something he had to adjust to. He's got used to that kind of lumping together of all writing, just as he's got used to the way people pigeonhole him now as a Serbian writer. He has to accept that, and has nothing against it, but he rightly feels he is in the company of great writers like Ivo Andrić, Danilo Kiš, or Milovan Djilas when he is seen as a Yugoslavian writer. To many, he is still considered a Yugoslavian writer because he is in communication with writers from all over the former Yugoslavia, and he regards himself as very much a part of that circle. Yugoslavia is no longer one country, but he isn't to blame for that, and he feels good in Croatia, in Slovenia, and in Bosnia. He happens to have been born in Kosovo, because his father was working there as a doctor after the war. I understand what David means about feeling comfortable with all the component parts of his former country: I feel comfortable in both the major cultures of my country—the English and the French. But I regret that I don't speak, read, or write Chinese. I regret not knowing what kind of person that Cantonese part would have represented. When I go to Hong Kong, I am enchanted by it, even though it is a terrifying machine of urban display. When I retrace the paths of my family there—Repulse Bay, the Peak—I feel more than nostalgia, more than regret. I feel the total loss of something important. I know my family on both sides has been uprooted for three and four generations, but none of them ever lost their language, and the older I get, the more I regret that I lost mine.

David's parents made a decision after the Second World War to stay in Europe rather than emigrate to Israel. And so, an early displacement did not happen. He came to Canada instead much later in his life. He understands his role as a writer with great clarity. He knows what the borders of the world of the writer are, and he knows that if you cannot express something, it does not exist. He says that it is magic in a certain way, because you can use words to create something out of nothing. Each creation, each story, each book, is a miracle.

Above all, David does not see himself as an exile. He told an audience in New York recently that he believed in Joseph Brodsky's notion that an exile is somebody who goes to something worse than his or her original position. He did not. He feels that in Canada, diversity has reached perhaps its highest level. On a practical level, diversity has had its effect on Canadian literature, and that, he says, is "really beautiful, because all these different [people] bring their histories to Canada. Canada is a sum of different histories as well as having its own history. The history of Canada is becoming more and more universal through its literary voices who have come from all over the world." He knows that reading the work of someone who lives in Canada but writes about a situation in Kashmir is different from reading the work of an Indian writer in Kashmir writing about the same subject. He feels that belonging to Canada while still being part of your country of origin helps writers like him reach readers in a unique way. I am certain that he is right and that it is something we haven't totally fulfilled yet in our literature. We are the sum of all kinds of traditions. We are able to absorb them and make something new of them because we have given people the peace, tranquility, and, often, the economic security to write about what they want.

When David's son, who had just graduated from university, announced he wanted to return to Serbia, David was astounded. After making the adjustments necessary to live in a peaceful society as far as possible from the chaos and turmoil of Serbia, David could not believe that his son wanted to go back. But his son packed his bags and went back to be involved in the new European politics. There is nothing that David and his wife can do about this, but they are obviously concerned. As he discusses being a Canadian with his daughter, he realizes that she feels fully and unequivocally Canadian. In a family discussion once, she let drop the phrase "you immigrants." He asked her rather sternly, "What do you mean, 'you immigrants'?" And she replied, "Well, I'm a Canadian." It was then that he realized how different her perspective is, how her road is not the same road that he and his wife travelled, and definitely not the one his son has chosen.

Listening to what David says in public, and in reading his work, you realize that he is constantly on a path of discovering who he is. In his novels and particularly in his short stories, the figures of the mother, the father, and the son are very much reflections of his own life and family. To say they are fictionalized makes it sound as though they are somehow trivialized. This is not true. He has been able to use his family, and the reality of what has happened to him, to achieve a greater discovery. He writes:

> Each one of us is our own dream that no one else can dream. No one but artists. They are the only ones capable of crossing unnoticed the line of separation between reality and dreams, to visit the sleeping and then to announce to the ones wide awake—by words or images, by sounds or voice—what they have learned in the world behind eyelids. If there were no artists, we would probably exist in a world without dimensions, like shadows dreaming of other shadows. Thanks to artists, the world is presented to us in its completeness, in the fullness that we would not notice otherwise …
>
> In other words, artists … paint their dreams, and their paintings, like windows, open up the passages through which we enter our own self, discovering the true face of the world. We are the world, the world is a dream, the dream is a picture, the picture is us. The circle is complete.

Reading Albahari's work and talking to him makes you understand that he has developed a creative tension between his identity as a Serbian writer and the person who came to Canada. In Canada, he was able to escape pressures that were inexorable, particularly the pressure to be more politically engaged in Serbia. As a writer and as a citizen there, he would have been more vulnerable. Leaving his homeland has not been terrible for him, because his voice is still heard through his books. He sometimes asks himself whether the writer has more rights or obligations because of being a writer, but he realizes that the writer has the right to make mistakes just as everyone else does. Ultimately he knows, as all good writers do, that he will be judged only on his work.

Interestingly enough, even as he writes in Serbian while living in Canada, David feels he is obligated to speak to everybody. He does not comfort himself with any particular ideology. All he wants to do is write. Writers, he says, communicate in a kind of universal language that gets translated into the individual languages we happen to use in this Tower of Babel. He knows his writing will mean different things to different people in different parts of the world. The fact that he is writing in Serbian, the language of some fifty-five thousand people in Canada and about twelve million in the world, makes him feel that he must write for everyone, no matter where they come from.

It seems to me that Canada is able to give writers like David Albahari the freedom to reach the widest kind of audience possible. In David's case, the themes have become universal because he has been able to use family figures—mother, father, child—in a way that extends beyond exploratory autobiography. He has pushed the limits of what we can understand about those roles, psychologically and emotionally, having been freed from them to a great extent, and freed from his own history, by coming to Canada. He has come to realize and to make his readers realize that if you understand "what is going on inside a family, you are going to understand what is going on in the world." Patterns repeat themselves, only the scale is different.

Strengthening David's work as a writer is his work as a translator of other writers into Serbian—Saul Bellow and Thomas Pynchon, among others. This has made it possible for his mind and psyche to undergo a metamorphosis, because, as he says, "When you translate, you have to transform yourself. You have to become the writer whose work you are translating in order to find the best solutions in your own language." And to search how somebody else's mind works through their own literature, to sense the struggle, to find the right word and then to translate it, is an enriching experience. He calls it "listening to a lecture on creative process." Naturally he follows the rhythms of the English language and puts them into Serbian; he develops a sense of the nuance of language and he becomes "more aware of the power of language to create and sometimes to destroy the world."

As a translator and even more as a writer, David is able to project himself imaginatively into the experience of the other. This has become part of him now in all aspects of his life. He told me,

> I myself cry often—I cry when I read in the morning papers
> about some terrible accident that took several lives ... The
> last time I cried ... I was reading an article in the papers
> about how people living in an area in Calgary refused to
> allow a methadone clinic to work in their neighbourhood
> and threatened its doctors and nurses. I thought of all the
> desperate men and women suffering from addiction to

different substances who will be hurt by that decision—and
I cried.

In David's novels, the themes of family unhappiness, the helplessness of the individual caught in the web of history, are part of his humanity now. They are not simply themes for elegantly constructed writing. David Albahari's universe expanded unexpectedly because he came to live in Calgary. He has not just taken refuge: he has expanded his universe and been transformed.

SPENT BY
GOOD AND EVIL

I made my first trip to South America in 1987. Well, not really. I had been to Rio de Janeiro when I was two and a half on the *Gripsholm*, the Red Cross ship that brought my family from Hong Kong to New York, from where we entered Canada in the summer of 1942. I have no memories of Rio de Janeiro, but the city marked both my parents forever. My mother always used to say she wanted to return to Rio and really learn how to samba. While our ship was docked there, she and my father had explored the town a bit and dropped in to some cafés where couples were dancing this Brazilian dance. They both loved to dance, and this became the one happy moment in a perilous and uncertain journey. They frequently recounted this story, and it somehow symbolized the optimism and unquenchable spirit of my mother and my father. They were very different from each other, but they shared a keen certainty, which I have inherited, that some of the most frivolous things in life are the most important. I believe there was also a pair of alligator shoes and a handbag that my father bought for my mother. It seemed to me this scenario—two people heading into the unknown with two small children and taking the time to dance the samba and buy alligator accessories—illustrated my parents' optimistic tenacity.

For me, the idea of South America had always been exciting, but my work in television rarely took me there. Nor, to my great regret, had I learned Spanish. But I had a special interest in South America by the time I went there in 1987.

In September of 1973, the democratically elected Chilean government of Salvador Allende was overthrown in a military coup led by General Augusto Pinochet. To me, this was the formal ending of the liberation of the 1960s. Through academic friends, I had been aware of all the changes taking place in Chile with the election of President Allende and knew that many suspected the Americans weren't content with a Marxist government on the neighbouring continent. Many of us felt there would be some destabilization, but none of us foresaw the ferocity of the military coup. When it happened, darkness descended on a country that had ninety-seven percent literacy, a country of immigration like our own. Canada took in about thirty thousand Chileans who feared for their lives and had nowhere else to go.

Fifteen years later, in 1987, Pinochet's hold on the country was still strong, and I was involved with PEN Canada, the writers' organization for freedom of expression in the world. PEN was founded in Britain in 1921 to promote intellectual co-operation among writers, and with the rise of fascism and later communism it quickly expanded internationally. Early members were writers like H.G. Wells, Joseph Conrad, and John Galsworthy. It is apolitical and opposes any regime that seeks to silence people who wish to express themselves freely. It is a worldwide organization now, with 104 centres in 102 countries on every continent.

I have been involved with PEN since the early 1980s and have very much supported their activities, which ranged from simple grassroots efforts, like sending postcards to dictators asking for the release of writers they had jailed, to forging contacts at governmental levels and making investigative journeys. I was asked if I'd like to go as part of a team to look at what was happening in Chile to people writing for the theatre. The theatre was one of the places that dared the most to defy the regime. People like Antonio Skármeta had written audacious plays that could have been shut down, and sometimes were. But even dictatorships are sloppy, and they can't control absolutely everything.

So in the winter of 1987, I set out for Santiago with Bill Glassco, the founder of the Tarragon Theatre, and we met journalists and went to the theatre and met actors and directors who were being terrorized. One of the directors was celebrating a birthday, and there was a knock on the door. When he opened it he found a giant floral bouquet with a banner across it saying "Happy Birthday. This may be your last." On another level, if the regime did not like a play, it would pick up one of the actors in a car at the stage door, drive him around the block pulling out his fingernails or toenails, and then throw him back onto the street. Random terror and intimidation were the order of the day. Over two weeks, we gathered many stories like that. But we also had a chance to understand how deeply cultured a country Chile was.

There is an area of Santiago called Bella Vista, next to a lovely hill on which the house of the great poet Pablo Neruda stands. Bill Glassco and I were invited to visit the house, and for the afternoon we were simply left alone in it to look at his library, write letters from his desk, and prowl around his garden. Everything was just as he had left it. There were some Chilean

Canadians who had been drifting back to Santiago, and we made friends with them, as we did with a number of journalists who had all experienced degrees of difficulties. A magazine editor we met told us that one of his reporters was shot at the doorway of their office. There was an almost random air to the violence, which was not what I expected in a repressive regime. We tend to overemphasize the ability of totalitarian regimes to control everything. But their greatest strength is their ability to frighten us. It is fear that paralyzes us and makes us feel helpless; it is fear of retaliation for taking action that stops the action in its tracks. If I learned anything from the people I met in Chile, it was that if you could conquer that fear, you could start to conquer the control the regime had over you. At this point, there was no attempt in Santiago to keep the population in line. It was not obviously a police or army state. When we asked to visit the head of the secret police (whose job would have been hard to guess from his complicated title), we were accorded a gracious interview in which he assured us, with elaborate courtesy and a very large smile under an even larger moustache, that everyone was extremely happy in Chile and that economic development made the whole population feel fulfilled. I've searched in my notes to find the name of this gentleman, but I seem to have blotted it out. All I remember is an extremely clean and very large office, excellent coffee, and the total nonsense of our exchange.

The things I remember from that trip in 1987: the beautiful neo-colonial offices of the British American Tobacco company; goose-stepping soldiers; gazing at the Moneda Palace, where Allende's life ended violently in gunfire and smoke. I bought the recordings of Víctor Jarra, the popular singer who, along with many others, was tortured to death after thousands of suspected supporters of Allende were rounded up by Pinochet's forces and detained in the big football stadium.

Above all, I remember the sense of normalcy; it felt as if there wasn't really anything wrong here, as long as you stayed on the surface and took everything at face value. It was jarring to travel on the subway, because it had been built by the same company that built the Montreal subway, and the cars and the stations looked very similar. As I looked around the subway car, I saw the same mix of people you might see in Montreal or Toronto. This darkness had descended on a country that was so similar to our own. Chileans, like Canadians, were wedded to material comfort and a high standard of living, and they'd shared our New World sense that the future was something that you could have an effect on. Chile had the highest literacy rate in South America. This did not protect them. Virtually overnight the darkness of a coup and the death of democracy descended. I couldn't help but think that this could happen so easily in our country. What was so different? It was a chilling thought, and one that I keep with me to this day. I'm convinced that our profound roots of parliamentary democracy are what have saved us from militarism. Our tradition of egalitarianism goes back to the Magna Carta, and coloni- alism, in our case, provided an infrastructure that gave support to democratic movement rather than crushing it. We were lucky, too, in the personalities involved in our history: some colonial rulers, like Governor-General Lord Elgin in 1848, supported the reforms sought by LaFontaine and Baldwin and helped bring about responsible government and the democracy we have today. We never had chaos and revolution the way Chile and other South American states, like Argentina, did. Our pillars of parliament and the common law, and our acceptance of the complexity of English and French as languages and Protestantism and Catholicism as equal expressions of religion, equipped us to negotiate rather than fight.

In the late 1970s and early 1980s, I met many talented people from Chile through my television work and in the literary world. Many writers and poets took refuge here, and in Toronto or Vancouver there was hardly a social gathering where you didn't meet a Chilean or two. They added a richness to our lives here and spoke a Spanish that was different from that of Castilian Spain.

Shortly after we returned from our investigative trip, Pinochet announced he would hold a plebiscite to see if Chileans wanted a return to democracy. It seemed inconceivable that even a dictator could display such arrogance. He thought that if he posed the question, the Chilean people would choose him. I was busy with my television work on *Adrienne Clarkson Presents*, but I was determined to go back to Chile if they held the plebiscite. When the date was announced in 1988, I managed to find a francophone group from Quebec who were going as non-governmental observers. It was a wonderfully disparate group, including refugees, nuns, priests, and teachers, all of whom had a great deal of experience in South America. I was the least knowledgeable among them, but I benefited enormously from being with them for ten days.

We were billeted in an old school, and I shared my room with Thérèse, a former nun who had worked for decades in the poorest shantytowns of Chile. She was in charge of people who picked apart clothes made of wool and bundled the wool up to be sent somewhere to be recycled. She was humorous, down to earth, and taught me a great deal. We were prepared to do duty as observers on polling day. They needed women to monitor the women's polling stations because in Chile men and women voted in separate places. I think it was assumed that women would be freer to exercise their own will if their husbands weren't with them right to the very moment before they filled in their ballots. So Thérèse and I were part of the women's observation group. It all passed without incident, and of course Chile voted to return to free elections later in the year.

That night was very exciting; we were watching history. In effect, people were saying, "A mistake was made, and now we're going to make it right." That evening I met Ricardo Lagos, who would become the president of Chile some fifteen years later, and Sergio Bitar, who had written a moving account of being in a concentration camp with many others on a remote island named Dawson Island; at the age of twenty-eight he had been minister of mines in Allende's Cabinet. After he'd been imprisoned for more than a year, he was released when the Red Cross, Ted Kennedy, and former colleagues of his from Harvard University put pressure on the regime to let him go into exile. He went to Venezuela and started a shoe manufacturing business, which became very successful. But sniffing that democracy was in the air, he returned to his country, as many were doing at the time. The presidential elections were set for the next year. I returned for that event, and was subsequently invited to the inauguration of President Patricio Aylwin. It was then that I entered the Moneda Palace for the first time and saw the interior courtyard from where Allende and his government colleagues were shelled and attacked by Pinochet's soldiers in the coup. It was unbelievably exciting to be there and to realize that such a change could occur. There didn't have to be centuries of darkness. The light of democracy could take just fifteen years to reappear.

The approximately thirty thousand Chilean refugees we had received in Canada in the 1970s and 1980s had become very settled. Families had seen their children grow up, and Chileans were taking positions of responsibility in every aspect of Canadian life. We had members of parliament who were Chilean, and many published writers, and people working in television and at the universities. When the dictatorship became less vigilant in 1986—while still arbitrarily committing frightening acts, such as shooting journalists or terrorizing theatre people—many Chilean families decided they would visit and see how things were in the country they had left so precipitously. I think of this as a period of investigation of the place from which they had been exiled. There seemed a fair degree of flexibility about their return; whether they would want to stay became a matter of individual choice. Those who had struggled so hard to learn English and make their way quite often determined that their lives would be in Canada for good: their children had been born and brought up here, and they'd adjusted to their new country.

There is no question that among Chileans there is a terrific pull to their home country, but as things evolved in the next twenty-five years, it became evident to some that they could have it both ways and live in both places. Those who opted completely for Canada found that their life was inexorably changed.

The Chileans are one of those groups of immigrants who, due to circumstances beyond their control, came to Canada and then, when those circumstances changed, found that they themselves had changed. They had opened their eyes to another way of life. Female Chilean Canadians have talked to me about how they found Canada more egalitarian for women. Chilean Canadians show as a group what it is to have real choice: they have had the option of going home again. Many tried to do just that, and when they returned to Chile some of them stayed, but most finally opted for Canada.

One of my duties as Governor-General was to go on state visits to foreign countries at the request of the prime minister to further Canada's foreign policies. When I returned to Chile in 2001, it had been thirteen years since I'd last been there during the excitement of the inauguration of President Aylwin, and I thought of Neruda's evocative poem:

> We've lived through the ages with their bloody flavour,
> The smell of smoking rubble, of dead ash,
> We who were not able to forget the sight,
> Have often stopped to think in the names of God,
> Have raised them up tenderly, because they reminded us
> Of our ancestors, of the first humans, of those who ask
>   questions,
> Of those who found the hymn that united them in misery
> And now seeing the empty fragments where that man lived
> We finger those smooth substances
> Spent, squandered by good and evil.

Neruda died very shortly after the coup. He had been living outside Santiago at Viña del Mar on the Pacific Coast, which I had also visited in 1987. He had made his home into a kind of Ali Baba's cave of sea treasures—carved mermaids, fishing nets, old painted buoys. After Bill and I visited this second house, we really felt we had been Neruda's guests in Chile.

Again, on the state visit of 2001, I thought about the relationship among those of us who live in the New World. For one thing, we are all home to indigenous peoples that come from ancient civilizations. We are part of what has been here before we came, and we are part of what we have brought to these shores from our past. So the New World is not that new, as it welcomes the old. It has an endless past.

I felt on that visit that liberty does not ever stand alone or in darkness. It is lit by a surrounding mantle of democracy. Only the framework of democracy guarantees the respect of human beings for each other and fundamental freedom in all its forms with all its values.

Canada and Chile were both once colonial countries controlled by people overseas. We each achieved independence, although by different means. Canada and Chile have in common a sometimes hostile landscape, solitude, space, and remoteness. And then there is the diversity of our populations that have come from elsewhere and taken root in a new place. Neruda says that it is necessary for writers from the vast expanses of the Americas to fill its enormous space with their imagination. Writers, he says, have the fundamental critical obligation to communicate in an uninhabited world that is no less filled with injustice, punishment, and pain because it is uninhabited. He says, "We are called upon to fill with words the confines of a mute continent."

This was a significant trip for me as Governor-General because it linked the beliefs I have always held about human rights and freedom of expression with the reality of representing Canada's democratic tradition to a country that has struggled to return to democracy. We chose some extraordinary Canadians to accompany us. Among them were Roch Carrier, the national librarian, and Herménégilde Chiasson, the noted poet and painter (later the Lieutenant-Governor of New Brunswick), together with Victor

Rabinovitch, director of the Museum of Civilization, and Pierre Théberge, director of the National Gallery. We wanted to make a cultural impact, and I think we did. I call these people the dream finders, our voices. And we brought them not only from the cultural world but also from the scientific, agricultural, and business world so that we could show the Chileans a couple of dozen people who exemplified what Canada at its best can do.

One night, we were invited to use Neruda's house and exquisite hillside garden in Bella Vista, where Bill and I had spent a day in 1987. In the presence of Salvador Allende's widow, Chilean and Canadian writers recited poetry and sang music throughout the house. The Canadian poet and diplomat Emile Martel orchestrated an evening of memorable harmony. It was an extraordinary, beautiful culmination for me of what my relationship to Chile had been. And then the next day, when we signed an agreement with the Biblioteca Nacional de Chile to return manuscripts that had been written by Chilean writers in exile in Canada, my cup certainly was full. Roch Carrier made this gift to Chile's national library on behalf of Canada, and it was completed a few years later. The collection is a tangible literary expression of what it can be to hope and dream that liberty and light will return. As a reminder that perhaps I helped to play a small part in the process, the collection goes by the name of Proyecto Adrienne.

The Chilean-Canadian writers who lived for years in Canada have contributed their understanding of what our country can be. One of them is Nain Nomez, who observed that "like a nation a natural culture must be formed by the unity of diverse elements: it is the set of contradictions and encounters between them ... like any social process, culture is a plural phenomenon, a constantly renewed place of encounters and dialogue between the various cultural groups co-existing in a country." His colleague, another Chilean-Canadian exiled poet, Claudio Duran, says, "Exile and grammar each possessed / of its inexorable rule / like the polar flight of migratory birds that fall / in Lake Ontario / never to stop resting." The richness of the writing, the wealth of observation, the depth of understanding that the Chileans brought to us continues to feed us and has not yet been plumbed to its depths.

8

Tamara Toledo

A woman in her late thirties sits across from me in a crowded French bakery café on St. Clair Avenue in Toronto. Her name is Tamara and she is eight months pregnant. When her mother was pregnant with her, she was tortured. Tamara reminds me of many of the Chilean women I met when I visited Chile in 1987—dark hair, milky-white skin, large dark eyes. She has quite a successful career now as an artist and works on a large scale, painting diptychs and triptychs featuring human features, mainly female, with large, dark, tormented eyes. She shares a studio with a number of other artists in a municipal space created out of old streetcar barns that also houses an organic market and community groups. I have found her through my photographer friend Rafael Goldchain, who is originally from Chile. Rafael is a renowned photographer in Canada now, his last notable show being a series of portraits of his ancestors, both male and female. The portraits feature Rafael himself playing each person, dressed in clothes of the appropriate period. He went to Israel at a time of difficulty in the Allende period and therefore is not part of the story of dispossession and diaspora. But he has introduced me to Tamara, and we have an exchange that is deeply moving and disturbs me for many days afterwards.

❦

The brutality of the repression by the Pinochet forces after they seized power in 1973 and the use of torture against the population was well known. I felt a particular sensitivity to this situation, as I had grown up hearing my parents speak of the Japanese occupation of Hong Kong under which we lived for six months in 1942. At our cottage on McGregor Lake, Quebec, in the long summer evenings, they told their friends about the terrible things they had witnessed. The light never seemed to fade at McGregor Lake, and the view of trees edging the water contrasted with the violent picture they were describing. I remember pretending to be asleep (I was probably about ten or eleven), because I did not want to hear these stories ever again. I remember my mother telling me that she knew of a woman who was raped by a Japanese soldier. With a group of his fellow soldiers, he had looted her apartment, and after he raped her, he threw money down before he left. I don't know why the detail of the money disturbed me more than almost anything. It had obviously made a huge impact on my mother. There were times when I wondered how they could sleep at night when the stories they told were so vivid. They had known people to whom these things had happened, and they, and the people, had survived. To me, the message seemed to be that you could survive anything if you decided you were going to.

Rape as an act of war was something I was conscious of before I knew about the so-called facts of life. It seemed to me then, as a child, that this violation was something real and widespread. I knew that my mother had dressed as an old woman when she moved from hiding place to hiding place with my brother and me. My father was in the Royal Hong Kong Volunteers, fighting beside the Canadians and the British. The entire island was a battlefield and then a conquered city. There was even a picture of my mother in wire-rimmed glasses with her hair pulled back in a bun, attempting at twenty-six to look twice her age. Once, the Japanese, looking for young women, burst into a basement in which we had taken refuge and found my grandmother playing on the floor with my brother and me. My mother was hiding in the cupboard. I have always identified with her shaking with fear in that closet. Later, in my adolescence, when depression and sadness overcame her, I even wondered if perhaps that story had been doctored so as to spare us children; that perhaps she had been pulled out and the worst had happened. When my father was eighty-five and I was fifty-five, I asked him, finally, if that could have been true, and he responded immediately and emphatically that it was not. I asked him how he could be so sure, and he replied that if that had happened to her, she would have killed herself. When I consider the way in which my mother approached sexual matters—matter-of-factly and often with humour—I think I have the answer that she actually did escape that horror.

And then I think of what I must have internalized from that episode. Do I remember the banging on the door, the shouting, the four or five soldiers filling the small room? That my brother and I didn't cry out for our mother and run to the cupboard means that we were able to disguise our feelings, protect ourselves and her, and shut everything up tightly within ourselves. In *For Whom the Bell Tolls*, Hemingway has his character Pilar, a strong Spanish Republican woman who has protected Maria, the abused girl, tell

Robert Jordan, "Nothing happens to you that you do not accept." When I first read that, it had a terrific reverberation for me; it was the story of so many women in Hong Kong, and it was my story in that basement when I was barely three. I have always taken it to mean that you can't go on living if you don't accept what happens to you.

When I met Tamara, she told me about her mother's experience and said she thought the opposite: that not remembering is a survival mechanism for anyone who has undergone a traumatic experience. Your mind can erase that memory and so erase the experience. That is what happened to Tamara's mother. She had found a haven in Canada, returned to Chile after ten years, and then returned to Canada. And it was not until after all this, not until twenty years after her trauma, that she started to have flashbacks and remember what she had repressed for so long. The memories came back after she had a stroke and was in physical and psychological therapy. She had been pregnant with Tamara when she was arrested, blindfolded, and taken to a detention camp, where she was tortured and probably raped. Tamara knew only that her mother had had a difficult and unhappy childhood. It wasn't until she realized what her mother had suffered that they were able to develop a real relationship. It was as though the gaps had been filled in, and their mother–daughter bond emerged through the scar tissue of trauma and the horror of remembering.

Her mother and father were both student activists in 1973, like many in Chile at the time who were rounded up by Pinochet's army. It was a time of total repression, and most of Tamara's parents' friends, who were also students, were in prison. Many were killed. Tamara grew up in a family that was completely traumatized, with several of her uncles having been tortured and imprisoned.

Tamara was twenty days old and her mother twenty-four when in 1974 the family came to Canada. They were sent to Vancouver by the government, which placed refugees in different cities. They were very involved with the solidarity movement, which helped Chilean refugees get their own places and become settled. So Tamara, from the time she was born, was surrounded by people who had been traumatized by torture, detention camps, and exile. Often, she would think obsessively about the perpetrators of such evil and how she could assassinate them. She always wanted to return to Chile, because that's what her parents talked about at home. They wanted to go back as soon as they could, but they ended up spending nearly a decade in Canada before they returned.

When she was eight, in 1982, Tamara was able to visit Chile on her own to stay with her grandparents. She fell in love with her country. She fell in love with her new-found relatives, with the landscape, and with the culture. She had grown up in Toronto in a very tough neighbourhood, and the comparison made Chile much more attractive. Her school in Toronto had a diverse population, with bullying and the terror that children can inflict on each other, and she felt very left out. After protests in 1982 and 1986, the Chilean regime, under pressure at home and from abroad, was allowing some exiles to return, including prominent opposition figures. Tamara's parents were allowed to join her a year later with her little sister, who was then only two. But interestingly enough, it was very difficult for her parents. She knew other Chilean families in Canada who did not return because the children didn't want to go, but Tamara had always longed for it. It was a very curious experience to return to her country in the middle of the Pinochet dictatorship, with curfews and with the economy in bad shape. Her mother never found work, and her father had to open his own

small business, which never did very well. They were marginalized because they had left the country. And yet Tamara persevered.
She did projects on human rights in school, which was considered
rather daring at the time. But she had teachers who were left wing,
and she was encouraged and did well.

As a young teenager, she got involved with a boy who was
deeply politically involved and wrote pamphlets against the dictatorship. She would hide the pamphlets in her house for him. One
day, he turned up at the house because the police were looking for
him, and Tamara's family hid him and ultimately helped him to
escape to Argentina.

Things got really quite difficult for them as the Pinochet regime
imposed a new wave of oppression during the economic crisis. The
fact that Tamara's younger sister had been born in Canada made
it possible for the Canadian embassy to help the family to leave,
and they were taken to the airport by embassy people. When they
returned to Canada, they had the assistance of some people who had
been involved with the Chilean community and were able to find a
co-op for them to live in. Tamara kept her relationship going with
the boy who had escaped to Argentina, and even went back several
times to visit him there during vacations. As soon as she was able to,
at eighteen, she married him so that she could sponsor him to come
to Canada. She brought him back to Canada and finished high
school, and by then, in 1989, democracy had returned to Chile.
The marriage broke up after four years and she has lost touch with
him, but it is obvious he was the reason she remained so attached
to Chile. Even though the couple had been Canadian citizens for
some time, her longing to return to Chile had never left her.

Once she was no longer a teenager, though, she realized she
didn't really have much in common with the social attitudes in

Chile. She disliked the sexism and homophobia she saw there. Without realizing it, she had become Canadian. She feels it is now even worse in Chile, because the society, aping American consumer culture, has become extremely materialistic. The ideals she was brought up with and that Chile represented for her—solidarity, risking your life for other people—are not what she finds there now.

But what really changed Tamara was the birth of her first child. She was no longer a "nomad," as she puts it. Until her son was born, she never felt she had a real home. I can't help but feel that Tamara, who was in her mother's womb when she suffered such a terrible violation, came full circle when she herself had a child. Not only does she feel she belongs to her neighbourhood, but she feels she belongs in Canada. She is determined to give her two children (she gave birth to a girl while this was being written) the stability that she never had. When she was growing up, she would change schools almost every year. The family moved all over Canada. In Chile, she lived in the same house for five years, and she remembers it as the best time of her life. It is that permanence, and the sentimental attachment to her boyfriend, that made her so attached as a teenager. That's what she wants now so much for her children— that sense of belonging that she at last has found.

When pressed, she admits that her sense of belonging came very slowly. It began with her little family and her neighbourhood and now extends to her city and her country. But she still feels a stranger when she goes to a small town. It's not the wilderness that frightens her—as it does many newcomers with its unfamiliarity and vast size—it is the small towns. She feels very foreign in a small town, where everybody knows everybody. Even though she doesn't look different, she feels different. She feels a total outsider in the kind of Canada that is captured in Alice Munro's stories.

She was picked on at school, and she says her partner, now the father of her children, who is also South American and still has an accent, is discriminated against. She's quietly firm on this point. She says that prejudice and bigotry are hidden just under the surface in Canadian life. She knows it's the same in Chile, where people with an Indian background are discriminated against, and she identifies very much with the struggle of the Mapuche, who are indigenous people of Chile and Peru. When she lived in Argentina, she remembers seeing signs in Buenos Aires saying that Indians were not allowed. She says Santiago didn't have signs like that simply because it wasn't as blunt, not because racism doesn't exist in Chile. The notion of the superiority of European backgrounds in South America is still very strong, and she is disturbed by that. Tamara seems to accept subtle racism as part of life in Canada, but it has not held her back in her work as an artist. She is not exhibiting much now, concentrating instead on her baby, but she has an exhibit in the works for China.

Tamara believes that her generation of child exiles and refugees carries a special psychological burden because so many young people of their parents' generation, primarily university students, who were targeted by the Pinochet regime, were degraded and tortured in a way that traumatized them forever. The violence and brutality that took place in the Estadio Nacional, the football stadium where twelve thousand men and women were detained from September to November in 1973, was notorious. Tamara's parents and their friends saw their whole generation targeted, tormented, then killed or exiled. Their children, like Tamara, heard the memories of pain and loss and absorbed the persecution into their own beings.

Tamara believes many of her generation became apathetic as

a result, withdrawing into their own lives and families, refusing to get involved after having seen their parents politicized to the point of giving up everything. She feels that Chilean Canadians like her resented the fact that their parents devoted themselves to achieving political goals at the expense of their families.

Tamara and her family are not only like so many Chileans, they are like many other Canadians who have changed without realizing it. At one time, her parents thought that after the dictatorship they would spend six months a year in Chile and six months in Canada. Now they realize that they can't live in Chile any longer. With children and grandchildren in Canada, everything changed. In the case of Chile, a lot of the older people returned, but the children and grandchildren wanted to stay in Canada, creating a different kind of diaspora. Nothing stays the same and you cannot step in the same river twice. In Canada, we give people the opportunity to see what it's like to live here, but also to go back if they wish. They often find that it isn't just the river that has changed; they have changed.

Tamara has written a thesis for her master's of fine arts degree that looks at the uncertainty of exile and memory. In it, she quotes the filmmaker Luis Buñuel: "You have to begin to lose your memory, if only in bits and pieces, to realize that memory is what makes our lives. Life without memory is no life at all … Our memory is our coherence, our reason, our feeling, even our action. Without it we are nothing."

Tamara is an example of the difference between an immigrant and an exile. She counts herself as an immigrant now. She quotes the literary theorist Thomas Pavel, who has said that "Immigrants begin a new life and find a new home; exiles never break the psychological link with their point of origin." The anguish that many

Chilean exiles felt when they were allowed to return was paradox-ically rooted in the deep hope they had treasured for years that they would be allowed to return. More important, as Tamara points out, "Exiles thought of their own lives as secondary to the lives of the people who stayed and suffered in the distant homeland. Their memories, hardships and nightmares became a silenced knowledge, an absent memory that had no space for retrieval." The fact is that Tamara was present at her mother's torture. She was tortured with her, and she could not defend either herself or her mother. The mixture of guilt, helplessness, and identification makes for a very powerful cocktail that could have been destructive to Tamara, but somehow she seems to have escaped it with the creation of her own new family and her painting.

She feels that she internalized her victimization in the womb, because when she approaches a canvas and starts to paint her stark portraits of haunted eyes and rigid bodies, she does it from her subconscious. She recounted to me the story of a friend of her mother's who was in prison for over a year and gave birth to her daughter there and was tortured during her pregnancy. The woman's torturer would always play a song while he tortured her. When her daughter was about fifteen and they were listening to the radio together in Canada, that song came on. The daughter said to the mother, "Didn't you listen to this song when I was little?" The mother was in shock, because of course she had never once played that song. Tamara feels that her relationship with her mother has a depth and intensity that is not simply their filial bond. Even though memories came back to her mother during therapy, she does not know to this day how she was beaten, whether she was raped, if she was drugged or subjected to other humiliations. But in that stadium, everyone was subjected to horror; the women were separated from the men and must have absorbed each other's sufferings, hearing each other's cries and screams and pleadings. Her mother's amnesia masked the pain for twenty years, but it eventually had to come out.

Not very long after she was tortured, Tamara's mother went into labour and was taken to a hospital, where she waited in excruciating pain. Finally, she had a caesarean section because the umbilical cord was around Tamara's neck. Tamara was always told that it was a miracle she was born alive.

Twenty-two years later, Tamara's mother, having been in mental and some physical anguish for some time, sought the aid of a therapist. But eventually she had a massive brain haemorrhage that made her physically incapacitated to a large extent. When Tamara looked down at her mother in her hospital bed after she had had a dangerous operation to relieve the haemorrhage, it brought her to this reflection, which she included in her master's thesis:

> Whenever I see images of the 1973 Chilean coup d'état—whether it be of the four-hour bombing and siege of the Presidential palace, of bodies floating down the Mapocho River running through the nation's capital or of listening to President Allende's last radio address to the nation before his death, my heart begins to pound, my pupils widen and my body shivers. Bodily sensations remind me that the connections to such events are disturbingly familiar and are part of my present more so than of my past. The coup d'état has now become my mother's stroke, the Presidential palace in flames is now her bleeding brain, surgery is torture, paralysis equals curfews, memory loss is the burning of books, ambulances are helicopters, the hospitals ... torture chambers, the doctors and therapists ... military and state oppressors, seizures have become electrical shocks ...

patients are survivors, flashbacks are testimonies ... the loss
of a generation, the loss of vision is the loss of hope, loss
of short-term memory is the loss of the nation's collective
memory, stitches are wounds and scars my family has
inherited, censorship becomes silence and rehabilitation is
synonymous of the nostalgic return from exile and recon-
ciliation with my past ... the scars that the dictatorship left
on my mother's body, mind and spirit, are inevitably bound
to the collective health and politics of Chile.

It is obvious that the artworks Tamara has made in her exhib-
ition "Mourning Memory," images of suffering women, helpless
babies and girls, are her testimony to the truth of her own life and
the importance of documenting her experience and her individual
memory locked in the collective memory of the Chilean past. Now
she's part of an organization called the Latin American Canadian
Art Projects, which gives her a sense of passion, not only for the
art they are all creating, but also because she belongs to a group
who share a vision. She loves the idea of creating community, even
though she has to struggle with her responsibilities as a mother.

For Tamara, "the mere act of painting itself serves as a re-
enactment of my own body's fragmentation." And she says that is
why she paints "ambiguous environments, disturbing repetitions
and disconnected wounded bodies." It's evident from her work that
the narrative of her life has been torn apart by trauma. In producing a painting she is saying to the viewer of her art that she is still
actively involved in trying to survive. I find it extremely moving
that Tamara says in her thesis that she "acknowledges the challenges
imposed by reality [struggling] with the search for and construction of an identity, a transition from exile to artist that offers new
possibilities for continuity. The constant struggle to survive [that]

started at my birth is now accompanied by tools that enable a luscious colour dialogue with trauma."

Through her art, Tamara has striven to enter the memory of crippling trauma and bloody violence to gain control of it, to visualize and record it so that it can always be preserved. This she can now do because she has resolved the dichotomy of the exile who longs for home; she has learned that home is not where she thought it was, but here in Canada, where, when she sought safety and community, she was taken in.

A CANADIAN
ALCHEMY

We think of Canada as having been founded by anglophones and francophones. Some regard the battle of the Plains of Abraham as a final conquest. Some see it as part of a flow of history with an unfortunate bump in it. The details of what happened after 1759 are vague to most Canadians: the gist of it to most is that New France was conquered and Canada became anglophone, with a group of francophone Catholics forming a minority in a larger country.

After the conquest, small business people, artisans from the British Isles, Americans, Jews, came to Quebec and joined the farmers and the soldiers who had stayed and become farmers. The Anglicans used churches and chapels that had formerly belonged to religious orders for their worship—the Anglican church in Trois-Rivières, for instance, is a former Récollet chapel. In her two-volume history *The Anglos: The Hidden Face of Quebec City*, the writer Louisa Blair vividly recalls what the establishment of a Protestant minority in Quebec meant. The new Anglican bishop was horrified on his arrival in Trois-Rivières in 1793 to find his flock happily settled in the Récollet chapel, whose walls were "loaded with all the pageantry and … ornaments of Popish superstition … crucifixes, images, pictures of saints, altars, tapers and burning lamps." At the time, the Church of England, the Anglican Church in Great Britain, was very Protestant and allowed none of these things. But the new anglophone population in Quebec had to make do with places of worship as they found them.

In 1802, King George III granted the Anglicans of Quebec City a large sum of money to build the Cathedral of the Holy Trinity on the ruins of the Récollet monastery on rue des Jardins. It is the oldest Anglican cathedral in North America. Interestingly, many of the conquering British soldiers were Scottish and Catholic, among them General James Murray, Wolfe's successor, for whom Murray Bay on the lower St. Lawrence is named, and Malcolm Fraser, who also served with Wolfe at Louisbourg and Quebec. Fraser became the seigneur of the eastern part of the Murray Bay seigneury after 1759.

In the early part of the nineteenth century, there were bilingual and bicultural families as well. Louisa Blair tells us that between 1821 and 1854, more than half the girls at the School of the Ursulines in Quebec City were anglophone, and many of the francophone girls had attended English nursery school first. She tells us that Chief Justice Andrew Stuart and Lady Charlotte-Elmire Aubert de Gaspé were so bilingual that their parrot would speak to Sir Andrew in English and Lady Charlotte in French!

The non-Catholic population was swelled by educated middle-class Jews from Germany, the United States, and Britain from the mid-eighteenth century onwards. One Jew, John Franks, was appointed to public office as Overseer of Chimneys and was allowed to be sworn in on the Five Books of Moses "upon the faith of a Jew."

Probably, Jews were considered to be honorary Protestants; Blair surmises that some were likely buried in Protestant cemeteries. It was noted by an observer that minorities in Quebec were accepted in a way "inconceivable in the Old World." Indeed, when Franks swore his oath in 1768 on the Five Books of Moses and not the Christian Bible, he committed a public act that was not permitted until forty years later in Great Britain.

The British navy was the greatest in the world at this time and had an unceasing appetite for timber. Canada's riches in timber seemed limitless. All those British ships needed masts, and the wood for them came out of the heartland of Canada, down the Ottawa River, in rafts so large that dozens of people with thirty or forty little wooden houses on them could float on each one.

In 1810, a British timber merchant, William Price, arrived in Canada looking to procure wood for shipbuilding. The Napoleonic blockade had cut Britain off from the Baltic, until then a source of lumber. Price became involved in the trade that brought wood down to the St. Lawrence from tributaries such as the Ottawa River. Once the Hudson's Bay Company no longer had a monopoly, the land around the Saguenay River and Lac Saint-Jean was opened up, and Price developed the Saguenay not only by logging the raw timber, but also by milling the lumber, so that every little stream had a sawmill at its mouth.

One of his descendants, another William Price, expanded the company into pulp and paper, with the mill at Kenogami, north of Chicoutimi, becoming the biggest newsprint mill in the world in the latter part of the nineteenth century.

Pulp and paper was only one way of industrializing this part of Quebec. With the construction of a dam on the Saguenay, it was possible for the Aluminum Company of Canada (Alcan) to establish itself and for the Lac Saint-Jean area to be industrialized. By the time William Price (later, Sir William) dominated the Quebec pulp and paper industry, Quebec had become quite clearly defined along francophone and anglophone lines.

The chasm that grew between francophones and anglophones had a lot to do with the education system. The British North America Act of 1867 enshrined the idea of creating separate school systems for Catholics and Protestants. But in Quebec, these two religious groups had different reasons for staying apart. The Catholics feared that mixing with Protestants in a single school system would dilute the French language and weaken the clergy's grip on the populace. Protestants feared that the French-Canadian majority might extinguish their education rights. By 1869, with Catholics and Protestants having their own separate school boards, fewer and fewer Catholic and Protestant children mixed. The Irish added another wrinkle because they were anglophone but Catholic, and Jews were neither Catholic nor Protestant but were considered Protestant for purposes of education. All of this led to divisions that seemed logical and rational but had the effect of dividing a population that, in the eighteenth and early nineteenth centuries, had found ways of coexisting in a bilingual and bicultural way. Only in the last forty years has a return to the comfortable coalescence of that period occurred. The Blair family is an outstanding example of this evolution.

9

The Blair Family

Of the two official residences of the Governor-General—Rideau Hall in Ottawa and the Citadelle in Quebec City—it is the Citadelle that is unique, historic, and enchanting. A building dating from the period of William IV, it is part of the fortifications built during the War of 1812 against the Americans. Because it is constructed with deep and wide trenches where you expect a moat, it is frequently thought of as being the original fort of old Quebec. In fact, pieces of the old fort dating from the seventeenth century are scattered around and below the old hilltop, the site of intense excavation since 2004.

As a place to live, the Citadelle was an extraordinary experience. Overlooking the St. Lawrence, it is built in granite of severe but appealing geometry. Visitors enter it through an archway and a parade ground leading to long, low buildings of perfect Georgian proportions. There was a terrible fire here in 1979, and the archway in the inner wall was too low for the city's fire engines to get through; as a result, a lot of the structure was burned out. Thanks to the perseverance and good judgment of Governor-General

Edward Schreyer and the willingness of the government of Pierre Trudeau, the Citadelle was reconstructed with a splendid sunroom behind the famous terrace where Winston Churchill, Franklin D. Roosevelt, and Mackenzie King met to discuss the war and its aftermath at the Quebec Conference in 1944. It was an intense aesthetic and emotional pleasure to stand in the large windowed room, looking across the St. Lawrence River to the town of Lévis. We used it as a sitting room and a relaxed dining room. Guests in winter were always startled and delighted by the broken ice packs floating by, crushing against each other with the tide.

Historically, for new governors-general arriving by ship from Great Britain, Quebec was their first stop in Canada. As soon as they set foot on shore, they were sworn in. They went on to Ottawa by train, followed by containers of furniture and wagons of domestic servants, family, and their personal silver. As our governors-general tended to be members of the British aristocracy or close relatives of Queen Victoria, they usually had plenty of baggage. Quebec was much featured in paintings, photographs, and drawings as the place where British viceroys made their first acquaintance with Canadian territory.

I first visited Quebec City with my parents when I was about eleven, because my brother was taking part in a high school gathering of students from Ontario and Quebec. I remember being astonished by the old buildings, the historic feel of the place. It looked like something I'd seen only in photographs of Europe. I had never associated Canada, my own country, with this kind of history. Nor had I ever seen so many small stone buildings. Ottawa, where I grew up, was built of brick, with large blocks of stone used for ceremonial buildings. There were also a lot of wooden buildings in the poorer areas where our family lived, below Sussex Street. I was unprepared for the grandeur of Quebec, and I never forgot it. We went to visit the Plains of Abraham, where we joined a guided-tour group and saw the spots where Montcalm and Wolfe had both been mortally wounded. I remember thinking in a child's way how amazing it was that they should both have been on this field, so close together.

To me, Quebec City has always signified what is the oldest European part of Canada. It was very different from the Quebec I knew across the Ottawa River. We used to look over from Parliament Hill to Hull, and one of my earliest memories is of seeing the Eddy Match Company going up in flames and burning for days on the Quebec side of the river, where the Museum of Civilization is now. We would go across to what was then Hull to eat *patates frites* from horse-drawn wagons—an illicit gastronomic pleasure not permitted in puritan Ottawa, with its different health inspection rules.

Within three weeks of my installation, I went there for ten days and developed an instant longing—the hopeless idea that this could be the principal residence of the Governor-General rather than funny old Rideau Hall, which, like Topsy, had "just growed." It had been a long time since I'd spent more than two or three days in Quebec, and even then it was as a journalist, covering politics and language rights. Now I was in a place whose civilization was uniquely and spiritually Canadian.

At the Citadelle, I discovered a building that had five or six bedrooms and several reception rooms—a formal dining room and the huge sunroom giving out onto the St. Lawrence. The other half of the huge building was the mess and quarters of the 2nd Battalion of the Royal 22nd Regiment (the "Vandoos"), the famous regiment of my predecessor General Georges Vanier.

The first weekend I was there, I went to the Place Ste-Foy shopping mall because I wanted to buy a small shawl to put on a sofa and because I had not been to a mall in Quebec City. The girl behind the cash took my card, then looked up at me and said in French, "You're the Governor-General, aren't you?" When I replied yes, she said, "I'm very glad you're the Governor-General. I think it's wonderful, because you're an anglophone and you speak French."

I wanted to hug her. She summed up a good part of my life: becoming bilingual expressed a great yearning for me. I had enjoyed learning French; I had promised myself I'd do it when, at five years old, I was refused entry to French education because I wasn't Catholic. I had learned French because I longed to so much. I love the language and found a whole different aspect of my personality when I learned to speak and read it well. And now, here I was, a bilingual anglophone Governor-General of Canada, staying at the Citadelle, recognized by a bright young woman because I'd made the effort.

We, of course, wanted to meet people in Quebec City. At first, our circle was literary, because my husband, John Ralston Saul, had been published by Quebec publishers and had always made a point of going to the book fair in Chicoutimi, where I had accompanied him a couple of times. He had a large following in Quebec starting with his first book, *Mort d'un général*, which came out in Paris first in French and then was published in Quebec. We benefited greatly from his warm welcome in Quebec literary circles, and those were the first people we wanted to include in formal invitations to the Citadelle.

Then I spread my net a little wider and consulted my great friend Bill Glassco, with whom I had done a PEN mission in Chile. As director of Toronto's Tarragon Theatre, he had staged the plays of Quebec playwright Michel Tremblay in English. He was responsible for bringing a lot of Quebec theatre to the rest of Canada. Bill and I had been in graduate school at the University of Toronto together. I knew he had some Quebec roots, because his mother came from the Price family, of the Abitibi-Price pulp and paper company. Bill had returned to those Quebec roots in his later years. His mother was the daughter of Sir William Price, the legendary figure who owned the company that bore his name and until his death continued to go with his men into the woods to log. He was killed in a landslide with two of his men at Kenogami in 1924. Bill had bought back his family's summer home at Tadoussac, where the Saguenay and the St. Lawrence rivers meet. The house is a spacious, wood-panelled summer home typical of the late nineteenth century, on a street that ran along the waterfront called Bord de l'eau. Beside the bed in the guest bedroom was the pencilled note "Bill had a boy today," with a date underneath it, which had been scribbled there by Bill's grandfather. It was about Bill's birth, since his mother was also nicknamed Bill.

The house had been built by Captain Henry Fletcher, the secretary to Lord Dufferin, the governor-general of the time, who had built another house for himself at the far end of the bay. On the grounds of Rideau Hall, Captain Fletcher also built Rideau Cottage, which is still the residence of the secretary to the governor-general. We had visited Bill in Tadoussac many times, and he urged us to meet his closest friends in Quebec.

That was how we came to meet the Blair family. David Blair is a lawyer with a large practice in the city, and at the time he had three young children. One of his passions is the *course en canot* (canoe race) across the ice, which reaches its apogee during the Quebec Carnival, in which a team of five men cross the ice floes on the

St. Lawrence. They alternately row and jump out on the ice to pull the boat against the crushing ice. He partners his team with a Quebec family, the Pouliots, who are river pilots from Ile d'Orléans. It is gruelling, exciting, and dangerous. David has never won the race, but at fifty-five, wafer-thin, and muscled, he continues to participate enthusiastically. His father and mother, Ron and Minim Blair, also live in Quebec City, as do his sister Louisa and her daughter. Even though the Blair family had lived in England for thirty years, they had remained friends with, and been connected through work for nearly two hundred years to, the Price family. It is an astonishing story covering four generations of two families, and one that gives a great sense of hope about our country.

I love going to the Anglican Cathedral of the Holy Trinity, a delicate, Christopher Wren–like building in what is now known as *le carré anglais*, the anglophone square, in the centre of Quebec City. There are many other Anglo-Canadian landmarks nearby, including St. Andrew's Presbyterian Church, St. Matthew's Anglican Church, and the Literary and Historical Society, some of which go back to the eighteenth century. The cathedral is the oldest Anglican cathedral in North America; it has a pew for the governor-general, marked with the royal insignia. I never sat in it because that's not what I want to do in church, but it was an interesting historical artefact.

The Blairs were very involved in this parish—David was the chancellor of the diocese of Quebec, and three generations of Blairs sing in the choir every Sunday. As a parish, it is warm and welcoming, and although only two percent of the population of Quebec City is Anglo now, it still has a feeling of community. When I first went there, it had just begun conducting its 9:30 A.M. Sunday service in French. I could sense that this was a special place, the centre of a true community, one that wanted to be a part of everything that was happening in the city.

Meeting the Blairs was fascinating because they seemed to encapsulate the history of the anglophones who had remained in Quebec City, even if they weren't "Québécois pure laine." David is married to Paule Champoux, a francophone from a Quebec family, and they live a bilingual life with their three children. David and his sisters, Louisa and Allison, as well as their father, Ronald, believe that they belong in Quebec. Their family has been there for two centuries. This new generation is both bilingual and bicultural, and that evolution suits them.

After 1976 and the first election victory of René Lévesque's Parti Québécois, anglophones left the province of Quebec in droves, and there was much doom and gloom about whether any Anglo presence at all would remain in the province. But in the Blair family, it is evident that they are determined to stay, because Quebec is their home. They know their history of two hundred years, and they feel it not as a weight but as a gift and the tenderest of obligations. When Ronald Blair, who is now in his eighties, was growing up in Quebec City, there wasn't a single French Canadian in their circle of friends or even acquaintances. It was a Quebec City where the Anglo minority had power and mingled only with other Anglos. He remembers the one and only francophone family in his neighbourhood and recalls matter-of-factly that they did not really "see" those people.

Nowadays, a tourist might visit Quebec City and, judging by the historical plaques and statues, think that everything is franco-phone. At the Citadelle, a young francophone guide in historical costume plays the British general Wolfe, explaining his role with a French accent and without irony. The pipers of the 78th Fraser

Highlanders evoke memories of the momentous battle that shifted power so radically in North America, and they are francophone.

The Blairs were descendants on both sides from vigorous people from the British Isles. Ron Blair's maternal ancestors, the Marshes, a Baptist minister and his wife, immigrated in 1843. Their son William reconciled God and Mammon, starting a shoe business that eventually grew into an enterprise employing 1,500 workers. The mansion built on the money of the shoe business was sold years ago and is now home to La Vieille Maison du Spaghetti, a popular restaurant whose interior architecture still echoes the richness and wealth of a nineteenth-century industrial fortune. English and Scottish business acumen created sizable fortunes. Many French Canadians and the Irish lived in lower-town slums and provided the workforce. Louisa Blair, in doing research for her book on the Anglo presence in Quebec, came across an article describing her great-grandfather's abusive practices in his factories, employing children and paying them less than workers were paid in other cities. Unfortunately, exploitation of the newly arrived Irish fleeing despair and famine at home, and French Canadians seeking any paying job, was the norm.

The Marshes were part of an upwardly mobile group of immigrants who came with very little and found in Quebec a way to make their fortune, to make good marriages, and to join the Garrison Club, which still exists at the foot of the hill on which the Citadelle stands. It was originally a military club and now is a very much sought-after place to hold weddings and other receptions. In 1981, it broke down its barriers and admitted women as members. It is now ninety percent francophone.

The evolution of the Garrison Club is echoed by the evolution of an institution established with completely different values, the

Literary and Historical Society of Quebec. It was in great danger of collapsing before an appeal to save it was made by a number of Canadians such as Mordecai Richler. David Blair spearheaded the efforts to save the Literary and Historical Society, which is housed in the nineteenth-century courthouse, an architectural jewel dating from 1808. There were once dungeons in its basement, and outside there was a scaffold where people convicted of capital crimes ended their days. In 1865, the prison was closed and Joseph Morrin converted it into a college; the courtroom became assembly rooms. By the end of the twentieth century, the building needed millions of dollars of repairs to shore up the wall and keep the roof on. Both provincial Quebec money and municipal support were helpful in the restoration of this important part of the *carré anglophone*.

I often visited the Lit and Hist, as it was affectionately called, and loved reading in it. Its two-storey main reading room has a gallery and an astounding polychrome wooden sculpture of Wolfe in one corner. The whole place smells of books, the way the Boys and Girls House of the Ottawa Public Library smelled when I was a child and first fell in love with books. When David and Louisa Blair decided to preserve the building, it had the atmosphere of a colonial outpost in Burma, as Louisa says. And they could find a book that had last been signed out by their great-aunt forty years earlier. Over the years, the Blairs and a group of other citizens and the municipality raised money to restore the two assembly halls attached to the library. They are elegant rooms in the eighteenth-century, neo-classical style of Robert Adam, with five-metre ceilings. They have a curiously Jane Austen–like air about them; quaint dances and dinners could be held here. There is nothing like these two rooms, or like the Literary and Historical Society, in any other corner of Canada. Even in Halifax and

St. John's, there are no buildings that can boast this atmosphere of refined association, of elegant encounter. The proportions of the windows, the height of the ceiling relative to the length of the walls, put you physically into a space that demands a historical understanding.

To celebrate the reopening of the rooms in 2009, John Ralston Saul and I were invited to a large dinner with all the francophones and anglophones who had wanted this place to be restored, to be reimagined and used again as it once had been. I found it an uplifting and hopeful evening because it was proof that the two solitudes had been able to come together over something they both treasured. Louisa Blair has likened this anglophone and francophone side of Quebec to that of a couple who will always have their differences but who need to love and look after each other. She has put it beautifully by saying that love needs difference and that difference is found in those two communities, anglophone and francophone, in Quebec City. And it is manifested and understood by the Blairs and their friends. But this comes out of a history that is not all pretty. The anglophones took their power very seriously; they enjoyed it, they revelled in it. There was open prejudice against Roman Catholics and patronizing denigration of French Canadians.

On Ron's paternal side, the Blairs left Scotland for the very heartland of Quebec, le Royaume du Saguenay, the area we now know simply as the Saguenay. When I first went up the Saguenay River, which is a great fjord, to Lac St.-Jean, I felt I was truly penetrating a wilderness in a way I never have before. What must it have been like for the men of the Blair family to arrive there two hundred years ago, to see nothing but trees, the whales at the mouth of the Saguenay and the St. Lawrence? Robert Blair, Ronald's ancestor, had been hired by William Price to help raise food in this land isolated by snow and ice. For the area to be opened up for logging and other exploits, they had to be able to feed not only the communities but also the logging camps. Blair at first grew food to feed the workers. But his managerial skills were soon noticed by Price, and eventually he ran fifty mills for the Price family. It wasn't exactly enlightened capitalism: the workers were paid in tokens for food and clothes rather than in money. Louisa discovered in her research that this first Blair was much disliked. Apparently, he was extremely tough and driven, and was not averse to hitting his workers. In fact, he killed his own brother by hitting him on the neck with a saddle. It was called an accident.

The relationship between the Blairs and the Prices continued for four generations. Ronald Blair began working for them after university, spending two years in the Price logging camps and sawmills. Then in 1961 he was sent to England by the Prices to look after their interests there and took his whole family with him. It was very important to him that even though his children were growing up in England, they knew that their home was really in Quebec. He glamorized it, praised it to such an extent that they longed for it throughout their childhood.

All the children—David, Louisa, and Allison—came back every year to visit their grandmother. She could speak French but always spoke English first to let people know that she was anglophone. David ran away from his English boarding school, which he hated, but stayed in England until he came home at nineteen and entered CEGEP (Collège d'enseignement général et professionnel), which in Quebec bridges high school and university. He barely spoke French but longed to fit in. Allison also yearned to return to Canada. She insisted on keeping her Canadian accent and her hard r's. When Expo 67 opened, the whole family visited Canada, and Allison was even more determined to return. And when she did, she rejected many things about her Anglo background. She went to mass in Roman Catholic churches as a kind of rebellion against the attitudes of her grandmother and many Anglos of her generation. Allison voted for the Parti Québécois and refused to speak anything but French. David returned just before the first Parti Québécois government was formed in 1976; he loved the feeling of freedom and that he was learning a new language. The England that he had known as a schoolboy was uptight, old-fashioned, and rigid. He felt that in his native Quebec only his own imagination would limit him, and he got a job driving a horse-drawn calèche for tourists. He spoke French badly, but he was appalled by the other anglophones in his CEGEP class who didn't bother to improve their French and simply shrugged and said they'd be leaving Quebec anyway.

Initially, both Allison and David were captivated by the romanticism of Quebec nationalism. Allison got caught up in the dream of an independent Quebec and backed the separatists. David never flirted with separation, but he did want to understand what was going on in Quebec. He rejected the stereotypical view that Trudeau was a tyrant who was contemptuous of the francophone personality and destiny. He enrolled in law at Laval University and there met his future wife, Paule, whose francophone family were completely charmed by him; her grandmother said: "Il est tellement fin. C'est tellement dommage qu'il est Anglais." However, she continued to be charmed, and Paule and David were married.

⌒

The second referendum on Quebec independence, in 1995, was the hardest for David to bear. When he speaks about it, he has

tears in his eyes and uses words like "gut-wrenching." He couldn't
help taking the desire for separation personally as a rejection. He
resented the emotions that were stirred, and he felt targeted. As an
anglophone in Quebec, he felt he shouldn't have to apologize for
who he was. He admits that it nearly tore him apart. He was up until
two or three in the morning before the referendum, wondering if
he could stay in Quebec if the vote to separate succeeded. In the
end, he did not have to make that decision. Then in 1996, his sister
Louisa became pregnant and decided to return to Quebec to bring
up her child there. Allison, meanwhile, was working with children
in war zones and eventually moved to Burundi. But with Louisa
and David both in Quebec and settled, their father and mother,
after thirty years away, returned to live in Quebec City.

Now, three generations of the Blairs are together in Quebec
City again, and David's and Louisa's children are being brought up
bilingually. At least one of them identifies himself as francophone
rather than anglophone. The Blairs are now part of only two
percent of the Quebec City population, whereas their ancestors
formed fifty percent. But they have adapted. They have done what
they wished to do: live in the society of their ancestors and adapt
to the changing conditions. I find the Blairs inspiring because their
decisions are based not on ideology and not on a fixed position
of entitlement. Their forebears, the Marshes of industrial Quebec
and the Blairs of the Saguenay, would surely be astonished to see
their descendants become so bicultural and bilingual. The Blairs
closely identify not only with the land of Canada, but also with
the people who have been making and remaking it through the
centuries.

When you find yourself in a new situation, it is important to
understand the altered context in which you must exist. The Blairs

have had to reach that understanding, not because they came from someplace else, but because the context changed around them.

Living in Canada is not a static experience. It's a place fluid enough to hold many elements in suspension. This fluidity is our kind of democracy, which works as well as, if not better than, any in the world. We find ourselves suspended in that fluid with Aboriginals, francophones, anglophones, and all the others who have come after them. Occasionally, we have attempted to harm each other, but somehow we haven't been able to inflict too much damage. The wounds have not been grievous. The slashing blows, the violent attacks, are dulled by this fluidity around us. This isn't always appreciated by Canadians. The countries that attract us and helped shape us—the old nations, France, Britain, and, to a large extent, the United States—because of their mythologies make us feel we are somehow incomplete and soft because we don't behave like them, with battle lines drawn and final victory of one side over another. What the Blairs show us is that coming to this country with one language and one religion and then consciously choosing to become part of the other language and religion after two hundred years is an enriching adaptation. Civilization by increment is what we are about, and the story of the Blairs illustrates that. We can be more than we were born to be. We do not have to limit ourselves to one kind of personality. We can add dimensions. We can find outlets for every aspect of our individual and collective personalities. That is what it means to be Canadian.

With the federal election in May 2011, Louisa and David Blair differed over what a majority Conservative government would mean for Quebec and for them. Louisa was very glad that the NDP won so many seats in Quebec because it was the first time she had voted for a candidate who won. She was also happy that so many young people were elected. She doesn't want anyone ever to assume that just because she's an anglophone she would vote the way other anglophones and the rest of Canada might vote. She understands Quebec in her own way, differently from the way somebody from Toronto would. David, on the other hand, worries that the new Conservative government attained a majority virtually without support in Quebec and that this means trouble in the future. And he believes that even though the NDP encompasses many young people with social democratic leanings, the party may not really understand Quebec. He worries about Quebec becoming destabilized.

The Blairs want to live in Quebec, and they want to live as bilingual anglophones in a Quebec that is part of Canada. They bring together again a Quebec that existed in the first half of the nineteenth century, before the lines of religion, education, and language became rigid. They show that some anglophones are determined to claim a future in Quebec on the basis of their history and their desire to be a lasting part of Quebec, in both languages, both religions, and all of the culture.

FIRST BY BOAT,
THEN BY PLANE

In 1986, the German ship *Aurigae* dropped anchor off the east coast of Canada, putting 155 Tamil refugees in lifeboats to make their way alone to the coast of Newfoundland. Jammed into two frail crafts, they were asylum seekers fleeing persecution in Sri Lanka. They were finally spotted by astonished fishermen and brought ashore by Canadian officials, where they were met with sympathetic headlines in all the newspapers and with breathless TV coverage. I think many Canadians remembered the earlier similar scenes of the Vietnamese boat people and their helplessness on the high seas.

The Tamils who were on that extraordinary journey had made their way from Sri Lanka to East German Berlin. They had crossed to the other side of the Berlin Wall, and from West Germany somehow found passage on a cargo vessel manned by a German skipper. They spent two weeks at sea before the captain put them in lifeboats and set them adrift. These were human beings who had paid for their passage after making their way halfway around the world. They were originally allowed to stay in this country for one year, but it's safe to assume that all these Tamils have probably become Canadian.

It was the first time many Canadians understood that there were huge difficulties in the little island country of Sri Lanka off the coast of India. Many Tamils had been seeking to come to Canada since the 1983 riots in Colombo, the capital. The riots effectively ignited a civil war that lasted until 2009. It is now estimated that at least between eighty and one hundred thousand people died, and that probably half of these were civilians. As well, there are an estimated 1.6 million landmines in the northeastern part of the country, which was claimed by the rebel Liberation Tigers of Tamil Eelam.

It is difficult for Canadians to grasp the subtleties and complexities of a war that owes as much to the legacies of colonialism as to the conflicts between ethnic and religious groups.

Before Ceylon became independent in 1948 and subsequently took the name Sri Lanka, its population consisted of roughly seventy-five percent Sinhalese people and twenty-five percent Tamils. The Sinhalese are Buddhist and the Tamils are Hindu. Democracy was achieved in the post-colonial period, but as the political parties were largely drawn along ethnic and religious lines, the ethnic majority (the Sinhalese) were assured of power. From a technical point of view, democracy prevailed: there were political parties, there were elections, there were winners and losers. But the winners always came from the majority group. The Tamils of Sri Lanka felt even more under pressure with the passage of the Official Language Act in 1956. This made Sinhala the country's sole official language instead of English, which had been the language of the colonial legacy. This was somewhat modified two years later, when provision was made for the use of the Tamil language as a medium of instruction and for admission to the public service in the north-east of the country. However, the bitterness of exclusion continued.

Historically, there have always been Tamils in Sri Lanka; the island is only thirty kilometres off the coast of India, and the Indian province of Tamil Nadu is in close proximity. During the colonial period, the British brought more Tamils into Sri Lanka from India as cheap labour for plantations in the agricultural areas of the island. Many Sinhalese felt that the Tamils should be sent back to India, but most of these Tamils came to consider Sri Lanka their home. With bitterness and misunderstanding increasing, movements like the Liberation Tigers of Tamil Eelam, committed to full separation of a Tamil state, emerged. This separation movement led to the long-drawn-out civil war, thousands of casualties, and, inevitably, a huge desire on the part of the Tamil population to escape what seemed to be an impossible situation and look for a better life. Canada represents that better life.

Very few people are involved in the complications of politics in any country, but many are affected. In the case of Sri Lanka, the convolutions of its post-colonial period made life dangerous and, for many people, hopeless. Violence resulting in civil war along ethnic and religious lines claimed the blameless as victims in Sri Lanka.

From 1986 onwards, Canada received an increasing number of requests from Tamils for immigration and refugee status. Approximately two hundred thousand Tamils now live in this country, with the overwhelming majority located in Toronto and the rest in Montreal and Vancouver. After the Colombo riots, the Canadian government took Tamils into Canada on humanitarian and compassionate grounds, but at the same time required visas for all Sri Lankans, making it very difficult to get here legally. Today,

Tamils are still one of the largest groups of refugees seeking asylum in Canada. Although there is now peace in Sri Lanka, it's estimated that the war displaced six hundred thousand people within their own country.

In the last twenty-five years, Tamils have been making a place for themselves in Canada. Recently, one of them has leapt into the mainstream of our political life. Rathika Sitsabaiesan is a twenty-nine-year-old woman who was elected as a member of Parliament in the May 2, 2011, federal election in her first try for public office.

10

Rathika Sitsabaiesan

The young woman with the brilliant white smile has an early memory of her grandfather's house in the middle of a mango grove surrounded by the rich greenery of an equatorial landscape. I have searched her out because she has just accomplished something extraordinary: she became the first person of Tamil origin to be elected to the House of Commons, representing the Ontario riding of Scarborough–Rouge River. She is a Tamil, originally from Sri Lanka, a country formed by a mixture of races who follow Christianity, Buddhism, and Hinduism. Rathika Sitsabaiesan is part of the Tamil diaspora from Sri Lanka. Ethnic division and hatred in that country, as well as deliberate injustice, led to a quarter of a century of civil war that began in 1983 and ended only in 2009, when the Sri Lankan military defeated the Liberation Tigers of Tamil Eelam (known commonly as the Tamil Tigers).

Rathika is classically beautiful and carries that beauty with ease. In fact, everything about her exudes relaxed self-confidence. She wears a tiny diamond nose-stud and speaks clearly with excellent diction and a flow of language that shows an active mind. I'm impressed by her calmness, but also by her enthusiasm. There's a sense of purpose and determination that, if it weren't for her quick smile and flashing eyes, could be considered rather formidable.

We talk a bit about the Tamils in Canada: how most Canadians don't know there are also Tamils from India, that there is even an Indian state called Tamil Nadu, and that Tamils are primarily Hindu. The history of this region has been clouded by ethnic conflict, and it is very difficult for most Canadians to understand its nuances. Ethnic conflicts like this one sweep everybody into their orbit, and, like the situation in the former Yugoslavia, the conflict in Sri Lanka has brought suffering and displacement to different ethnic and religious populations as they've played the hideous game of taking turns at victimizing each other.

Rathika tells me some of her memories. She remembers how her grandfather helped her and her older sister learn English by naming the parts of their bodies. "Elbow" is the first word she can remember. He made a point of speaking to them in English because he thought that at some point they'd be going somewhere where they would need it. Because the official language in Sri Lanka was that of the majority Sinhalese, Tamils like Rathika's grandfather knew that they would have to learn English. And of course the British colonial period had stamped its cultural and linguistic patterns on the island. Rathika's other memory is of the house she lived in with her mother, her father having left Sri Lanka when she was just a baby. The house was at the end of a path surrounded by wood-apple trees, and the children would wait for the fruit to ripen so that they could eat them. They always waited for them to fall of their own accord.

Her mother worked as a seamstress in her own little shop, where she also sold a few groceries. She had a cow and some hens as well, and sold milk and eggs. There was a little room in the shop with beds in it so that her mother could stay there with the three children overnight if she kept the store open late. Another vivid memory for Rathika is of sitting in their little living quarters with her mother and grandfather when there was shooting outside. Violence was something they lived with, but her grandfather became very agitated, pacing up and down, and the children were told to be quiet, to sit down and not move a muscle. The people outside obviously saw some movement, because suddenly bullets were coming through the door. One landed right by Rathika's foot, although her sister says it landed right by *her* foot. And when they left the next morning, a body was sprawled out on their front steps. They thought it was a soldier.

When Rathika's father left Sri Lanka, he went to France to work. But when he found the language barrier too great, he moved to Montreal, using what little French he had to get himself admitted there. He had gone ahead to make enough money to bring the rest of the family over, a strategy repeated again and again in immigrants' stories. Most often, it used to be the men who came first, but now, with other immigrant groups, it is the women. The most obvious example is the Filipino women who come as caregivers, leaving their children and husbands behind until they have established themselves and can bring their families to join them.

This pattern has come to be taken for granted as a necessary hardship for immigrants. But how many of us can really understand the depth of the heartache and the emotional deprivation that such a step means? When my family had to leave our home under traumatic circumstances, at least I was with my parents and brother. It's harder to contemplate the situation of a mother who must leave her own children in the care of others while she comes to a completely strange land and looks after other people's children or aged parents. It seems to me we are never grateful enough for the sacrifices people make to come to Canada. They come in the hope that they will have a better life—it's all based upon that search for a "better life"—but even if it works out economically, the emotional cost to families is great.

People seek to come to Canada not just for economic reasons but for the basic human needs common to us all: the need to feel secure, a sense of day-to-day well-being, and to believe that the future will be better. They do it to escape deprivation, low standards of living, lack of protection from the law, chaos in government, and violence. We have programs that help people who are entering the country for specific reasons, such as caregivers, and as a result these immigrants are allowed to sponsor their families to join them. I feel humbled by the tremendous strength and resilience they have; I believe their sense of family is particularly strong because of the lack of legal and democratic structure in their home countries. It is this identification with family that I find most moving, and it helps us all remember that the basis for human nurturing and love lies in the family.

Rathika has a large extended Tamil family in Canada and abroad. When she was at university, she was very involved in the Tamil students' organization, and through the perseverance of her parents she kept her Tamil language.

She knows the sacrifices that have been made for her. When the time came for her mother and the children to join her father, her mother had to take careful steps to get them out of the country. In the chaos of a civil war, with uncertainty and violence on every side, they might have been the victims of extortionists. They couldn't tell anybody but their closest friends that they were making prepara- tions to leave. Once they were on the train to Colombo, Rathika remembers robbers yanking a chain from around her mother's neck. A woman alone with little children had to seek whatever protection she could find, and on their trip they were passed from safe house to safe house. Rathika never questioned where they were staying. It seemed that in this informal protective network they would just arrive somewhere and be taken in.

When Rathika was five, they flew from Colombo to Toronto. She saw a man waiting for them and remarked to her mother, "There's a man who looks just like Uncle." It was her father. He scooped her up and hugged her and everything was all right. For Rathika, that is what family reunification means. She didn't know her father, but she knew about him and that he was waiting for them, and then there he was, hugging them in Toronto.

She hadn't really felt the lack of a father because uncles and grandfathers and other relatives were always present. They left behind the grandfather who had taught them English. She never saw him again because he died about eight years later; they brought her grandmother over then because she couldn't live alone anymore. Later, her maternal grandparents came, but they decided they couldn't live away from Sri Lanka. Rathika remembers them as being very much in love, even though they were old—and so it seemed, because her grandfather died of a broken heart shortly after his wife died. Rathika now has her one paternal grandmother in Canada; when Rathika won her riding, her grandmother's first question was "By what margin?" Her English had been quite good when she arrived in Canada, but after living with Rathika's family and then moving to her son's when he had children—she wanted to be where the babies were—she lost a lot of it because they generally spoke Tamil at home.

Rathika feels she is surrounded by family, not only her

grandmother, parents, and siblings, but also by first, second, and third cousins, even if some of them live in France and Germany. In the aftermath of the civil war in Sri Lanka, she and her family don't know whether certain relatives are alive, whether they were caught up in the conflicts, whether the children were conscripted to be child soldiers, whether they lost their homes.

Fear has been a large factor in her family's life. Not just the fear of physical violence, of riots, shootings, and acts of war, but the fear that they couldn't manage their own lives, set their own goals. Her mother, whom Rathika characterizes as brilliant and fearless, had earned a full scholarship from her school to go to England to be educated as a doctor. But because her older sister had married at thirteen, she was in charge of the family after her mother died, and she couldn't accept the scholarship. Instead, she worked to keep the house, cook all the food, and ensure that everyone was fed, even though sometimes there was nothing left for her. She'd just drink water to still her hunger and then go to school. She was also a star athlete and a senior prefect with the highest grades possible. Nobody realized the strain she was under. Although her mother's dream died, Rathika carries that dream within her. And that, too, is very common with immigrants. The first generation has experienced loss and failure, but they imbue their children with the knowledge that they can have a dream. Rathika's parents lived their adolescent lives knowing they would almost certainly have to leave their country as adults. They accepted disruption and loss as their fate and gave themselves the goal of finding the right place to go.

Rathika believes she has always been an independent person because that's what her parents prepared her to be, shaping her for an unknown future in a foreign country but knowing it would be better, no matter what, than Sri Lanka.

She knows she couldn't possibly have been so independent had she been living in that house with the mango grove. At the age of seven, she had her first taste of community organization. The family was living in a little apartment in Mississauga, just west of Toronto, and had no money and no car. But it was very important to Rathika's parents that she retain her Tamil language while getting used to Canadian society and going to English school. Her father found a Tamil-language class in Scarborough, and he took her there every Saturday morning. It was on the far side of Toronto, so it took them hours to get there and back by bus, but she counts herself lucky that at least they found one. Her father would take the four kids, and the next year a neighbour included his three children, and for two years they kept this up. When it became too much, seven-year-old Rathika and her father contacted the public school board and requested Tamil classes closer to their home. The school board declined, so they approached the Catholic school board. The Catholic board agreed if they could sign up thirty people. That was Rathika's first demonstration that the democratic system worked. They got the registration forms, pasted the neighbourhood with flyers advertising classes, knocked on doors. And they got their Tamil classes.

That was seventeen years ago, and it was the start of a thriving program of various language classes called the International Language Program. The Tamil program grew quickly over the next few years to six or seven classes at ten different sites in Mississauga. Rathika was a student in her father's class, and once she graduated, she went back as a volunteer helper and then began working at the school as a clerk in the office. When she went to university, she became an instructor. Her father had never taught anything before, but he barrelled ahead and did it because it had to be done. Rathika discovered that she had a natural ability to teach and eventually in university she got her certificate to teach English as a second language.

Twenty-five years ago, Mississauga was a very white place. Some kids called Rathika "dirty" because her skin was brown, and they rubbed her skin scornfully. She generously says that they didn't understand and doesn't seem to hold any resentment towards them. Of course, what she's describing is racism at its most basic and ignorant level, but it never stopped her from doing anything; it obviously never stopped her from feeling good about herself. She says her mother's strength has always given her the drive to keep going.

Early in Rathika's childhood, when her father was working in a door factory, he was thrown off a rotary machine and landed on a wide metal bar. The accident crushed three discs in his spine. Luckily, he still had some mobility after lengthy surgery, but for long periods of time he was unable to do anything. After half an hour, he needs to change position, and he can't walk for more than thirty minutes. Rathika's mother had already signed up to do a six-month course to be a registered practical nurse. She'd been interested in medicine since her early dream to be a doctor. When her husband was injured, she knew she couldn't go back to school and look after her children as well. Rathika's father was insistent that they would not go on social assistance. He felt there was a stigma attached to it; they *must* be able to look after themselves. So her mother gave up another dream and found a job in a warehouse that ships goods for different manufacturers. She was fortunate, because it was a union-ized job with benefits and the reassuring knowledge that being laid off didn't mean losing her job permanently. Rathika's father was on workers' compensation then, which didn't pay enough even for rent. Her mother became the sole breadwinner. Twenty years later, her mother still works in the same warehouse.

When Rathika's uncle came to Canada, he lived with them and they were able to rent a house. She always remembers at least one extended family member living with them. Some Tamil houses were really community hubs, and Rathika's parents had one of those homes where everyone was welcomed. They took care of anyone who was brought to them. Rathika learned from her parents' example that giving to the community and helping to build up other people was a good thing. Even when they had very little, they were always willing to take on other people to help them feel comfortable, feel at home even in a foreign place, until they could go out and get a steady job and stand on their own feet with some pride. Often, steady jobs were hard to find, but it always seemed to work out, eventually.

Rathika became a strong and physically active girl, climbing trees and playing football with the boys. She plunged into activities at her school, and starting in Grade 6 was on every single sports team. She felt she really belonged when she played sports, and that the more involved she became at school, and the more involved she became with her teachers and guidance counsellors, the more at home she felt. Her older sister looked after her in school at first, but when her sister went to another school, Rathika turned to her teachers, who were pleased to help a bright, promising, and outgoing pupil.

When Rathika explained this to me, I identified with it very strongly. I, too, had looked to my public school teachers for guidance and as models, and each one of them is clear in my mind as having been encouraging. I remember telling my Grade 7 teacher, Miss Jackson, how much I liked to read, and two days later she asked to see me after class, whereupon she lent me her own copy of *Jane Eyre*. She gave me a very solemn look and said, "I know you will love this book as I did. But I don't want you to tell anybody that I lent it to you, because I wouldn't want them to think I had put inappropriate matter into your hands." She was right: I adored the passionate love story of Mr. Rochester and Jane Eyre. I think we owe a great deal to our teachers in the public school system for understanding and helping new Canadian children. Those children want to learn everything and to take part even if they can't fully understand it all, and even if their parents have very little idea of the feeling of belonging that a schoolteacher's attention can give to an immigrant child.

Rathika liked her teachers so much, she never corrected their pronunciation of her name, which put the accent on the second syllable: Ra-*thee*-ka. It wasn't until she got to university that she was bold enough to tell people her name was actually pronounced *Rath*-ika, with the emphasis on the first syllable.

In Grade 5, when she was ten, at her teacher's suggestion, Rathika started to volunteer at a nursing home in Mississauga where the residents didn't have many relatives who came to visit. She would play card games with the seniors and watch television with them and generally just chat them up. She loved doing that and felt it was important because they were very isolated. She always felt that they enjoyed her company and were entertained by her. She would do exercises with them and they'd go for walks, and by the time she was in Grade 8 she was organizing a weekly bingo game for them. When Rathika told me this, I realized that a child brought up in such a large extended family, or in a household where people in need are treated like family, is at a tremendous advantage in working in the community because everybody is considered part of the group. No one is excluded. So many individuals who come from a so-called underdeveloped country where families are important are able to relate to a very broad range of people. This openness comes by being surrounded by others in a community, and being aware of what unites you, not what divides you from one another.

Rathika's parents enthusiastically supported her community activities and drove her to sports practices after they got a car when she was in Grade 6. But she didn't tell them she was dating until after she had started Grade 12. They weren't pleased, but they were consoled by the fact that she was set on going to university, which was their goal for their daughters. Rathika wanted to go away to university in order to be independent, and in Grade 10 she started preparing her parents. When she was accepted by Queen's, her parents agreed that she could go. Unfortunately, she began to develop very bad migraines, so bad that she was hospitalized. Her mother then insisted that she stay at home and go to the Mississauga campus of the University of Toronto. By the time she was in her final years of high school, she was doing co-op at Mount Sinai Hospital, where she continued to work during her first two years at U of T, because it was still in the back of her mind that she would become a doctor. But eventually she realized she didn't want to put in thirteen more years of education before starting out in the world. She decided she would switch to Carleton University and get a business degree. She immediately started working at the students' union at Carleton and became the vice-president in her second year there. She says she was "the first brown woman to run and win an election at Carleton."

She's very offhand and detached when she talks about racism. She says she accepts that it exists and moves on. What she distrusts is people saying that they "don't see colour," because her sensitivity makes her feel that's a mark of racism. She feels that it is important to recognize that you are different and not dwell on it: "It's funny, when people hear me speak, they say, 'But you don't have an accent.' And I'll say, 'Okay, you are expecting me to have one, why? Even though you knew I grew up here and all my linguistic training was here. Why would you expect me to have an accent other than a Canadian accent?' And then they'll say, 'Oh, but you're Tamil.' And they'll say sometimes, 'Oh, you do so well in your speaking.' Oh, wow! … What did you really expect? Because I'm young. Because I'm Tamil. Because I'm brown. I'm a woman and I'm pretty."

She knows she should have taken French-immersion schooling and makes a face when she says she regrets not becoming bilingual. But she's trying to make up for it now, and recently she took a two-month immersion course at the language school at Jonquière in the Saguenay area of Quebec.

When I ask her how she decided to get into party politics, she says she was interested in social justice and community development and looked around to see how she could become directly involved. Once she got involved with political campaigning and learned what each party stood for, she decided to plunge in. And it was because of her health-care background through her mother and her own education that she realized she wanted to throw her lot in with the NDP.

During the first campaign she was involved in, she went from poll to poll helping different candidates. She quickly recognized she had the ability to draw people out and talk to them and learned that she was good at resolving conflict.

When she was nominated by her riding in December 2009, she thought she'd be running against long-time Liberal incumbent

Derek Lee. She felt ready to face him. She's very tough and determined, and says she was ready "to pounce on him and beat him and
win." Lee decided to retire when the election was called, however,
and the Liberals' seat was defended by a female candidate of Indian
origin. Rathika is very proud of the fact that the voter turnout
in her area went from something like forty-four percent in the
previous election to almost fifty-six percent. She believes she won
because her organizing made a difference and she reached out to
the people in her riding.

Rathika is bristling with energy and wants to make people feel
more engaged, using not only her experience with young people
in a students' union but also her experience of working with the
elderly. Because she's young, she wants to focus on civic engagement among youth and create a youth wing for her party in
Scarborough. She has her work cut out for her, because this is an
area that has not been known for its civic engagement. Her riding
includes her own neighbourhood of Malvern, which has a reputation as a tough place with youth crime. But the Metro Toronto Zoo
is also in her riding and the Rouge River has been declared a federal
park. It's an area usually referred to as "mixed," and in its shopping
malls and schools you see visible evidence that half of Toronto was
not born in Canada.

She feels that, for the most part, the Tamil community was
behind her, but that people from everywhere backed her because
she has been an advocate for human rights and social justice. One
of her constituents told the *Toronto Star* that Rathika won because
"she's brilliant ... and brave." But not all of the Tamils were for her;
many worked on the Liberal campaign and on the Conservative
campaign. Still, she got a lot of support from people who would
say, "You're like my grandchild. You're like my daughter. You're like

my older sister." She feels buoyed by the fact that Tamils are proud of her. Her parents still live in Mississauga and worry about her living on her own in faraway Scarborough, but she has managed to keep them calm.

Rathika says that many in the Tamil community are very politicized because they were forced to leave a country that for two generations suffered from civil war and unrest, but that others want to disengage when they come to Canada; they've already had too much politics. She wants to show them that politics is different in Canada: constructive and inclusive. She also wants to build on those who will do anything to help Tamils in their community. The Tamil community is not a monolithic one with just one button to press. Also, as a community stays longer in Canada, its values and its attitudes are bound to shift. Rathika identifies with other women who come from the Subcontinent—India, Pakistan, and Bangladesh as well as Sri Lanka—and she realizes that it is mostly women who really keep things going. She sees women as a great source of strength, having drawn on her own mother's perseverance. Women have had to draw on deep wells of endurance no matter what. She is keen about getting other women from the communities she knows—Filipinas, for example—to run for elected office, because that's how we'll be properly represented in our parliaments and legislatures. She is the voice of the newest of Canada, and that voice is strong, loud, and clear.

TOMORROW IS ANOTHER DAY

It is both uplifting and perplexing to learn the stories of people who have lived lives of risk, deprivation, and violent reversal. Naturally, the triumph of one human spirit over adversity inspires optimism about our fellow human beings. But when you have had the experience yourself, there is something that becomes unreal about it. If life is to go on, you must leave the experience behind.

Dwelling in the past, even if it is a past in which adversity was overcome, is not what the people you have met in these pages want to do. Their stories are their narrative, the path they have made individually in the forest of our collective dreams, desires, and destinies. In practical terms, their experiences tell us what immigrants who have known loss can contribute to Canada. They value and respect what we have created here: our system of democratic values, our historic biculturalism on which our diversity is based, our ability to change with technological and human advances. They have seen that by being willing to become whatever was necessary at the time—a cook when you've never cooked before, a laundromat attendant, a late-night disc jockey, a cleaner of hotel rooms—they were not diminished; they gained competence, assurance, and independence. A metamorphosis can be born out of deprivation and loss. I believe this is where the self-confidence is born that takes a little boy out of a refugee camp, or a hiding place among strangers, and puts him thirty years later at the top of his profession. And this story is repeated countless times by the 250,000 new Canadians who join us every year.

We have had a wonderful run until now in Canada. Our integration of new citizens has worked well, and through basic decency, a willingness to share our history, and an openness to the whole world, we have been the beneficiaries of the intelligence, skills, and family experience of people who want to settle here.

In the six years I was Governor-General, I travelled two hundred thousand kilometres a year to meet Canadians across this country, and the experience convinced me we have a solid framework for our burgeoning country, but the variety of what I saw also made me think with some anxiety about our future.

I was disturbed to hear from some the attitude that anything that happened in Canada before their arrival had nothing to do with them. To me, it is the equivalent of saying that the first Europeans arrived here to occupy and explore an empty land, as though the Aboriginal people were non-existent and their culture negligible.

Becoming a Canadian citizen is not like visiting a buffet table in a restaurant where you pick and choose what you want—a little of this, lots of that, none of something else. Canada has a set menu, offering, but not limited to, medicare, openness to immigrants, a just legal system. Neither is our darker legacy to be overlooked: we cannot forget the residential schools that sought to destroy Aboriginal culture, or the disgrace of dispossessing Japanese Canadians and transporting them away from their homes. When

Canada adopts you, you are part of the whole family, with its benefits and with its dysfunctions, with its birthday celebrations and crazy Uncle Herb.

None of the people in this book will ever say, "I don't want to know what happened here in the past, because for me history in this country began when I arrived." If our presence is to have meaning in our chosen country, we must all of us accept all our history. Our history must be taught and absorbed; our experiences, bad and noble, must be shared.

People said to my parents that we would be Canadians after a generation. We, as a family, never accepted that; we wanted to be Canadians immediately. I believe we must help new Canadians integrate and become part of mainstream Canada as soon as possible or we risk assuming the exclusionary ethos of European nations. I wanted my legacy as Governor-General to be the Institute for Canadian Citizenship, a foundation that helps new Canadians feel that they can penetrate our culture, discover our gift of a great natural wilderness, and benefit from and contribute to our infrastructure of democratic participation. Not all new Canadians can become Governor-General, but all Canadians can feel that the levers for full participation are to be found within their reach, that the doors will open for them equally if they turn the handle and push.

Having seen the deep generosity of our welcome to the Vietnamese boat people, I have always hoped that this could happen again, that we would see a need to save tens of thousands of people, not just to give them temporary refuge, but to reach out to them, as thousands of us did in 1979, and say, "We want you to be part of our world. We will make room for you. And you will become, like us, Canadian."

BIBLIOGRAPHY

Adachi, Ken. *The Enemy That Never Was*. Toronto: McClelland & Stewart, 1976.

Aga Khan IV. *Where Hope Takes Root: Democracy and Pluralism in an Interdependent World*. Vancouver: Douglas & McIntyre, 2008.

Appiah, Kwame Anthony. *The Ethics of Identity*. Princeton, NJ: Princeton University Press, 2005.

Bailey, Leuba. *The Immigrant Experience*. Toronto: Macmillan of Canada, 1975.

Blair, Louisa. *The Anglos: The Hidden Face of Quebec City*. Quebec: Editions Sylvain Harvey, 2005.

Brand, Dionne. *A Map to the Door of No Return: Notes to Belonging*. Toronto: Vintage Canada, 2002.

Buckley, Brian. *Gift of Freedom: How Ottawa Welcomed the Vietnamese, Cambodian and Laotian Refugees*. Renfrew, ON: General Store, 2007.

Daftary, Farhad, ed. *A Modern History of the Ismailis: Continuity and Change in a Muslim Community*. London, U.K.: I.B. Tauris, 2011.

Donskov, Andrew. *Leo Tolstoy and the Doukhobors: An Historic Relationship*. Ottawa: Centre for Research on Canadian-Russian Relations, Carleton University, 2005.

Farmer, Paul. *Pathologies of Power: Health, Human Rights, and the New War on the Poor*. Berkeley: University of California Press, 2005.

Fine-Meyer, Rose. *Unique Refugees: The Sponsorship and Resettlement of Vietnamese "Boat People" in Ontario, 1978–1980*. Toronto: University of Toronto Press, 2002.

Frankl, Viktor Emil. *Man's Search for Meaning: An Introduction to Logotherapy.* New York: Washington Square Press, 1963.

Hagan, John. *Northern Passage: American Vietnam War Resisters in Canada.* Cambridge, MA: Harvard University Press, 2001.

Kelley, Ninette, and Michael Trebilcock. *The Making of the Mosaic: A History of Canadian Immigration Policy.* Toronto: University of Toronto Press, 1998.

Kostash, Myrna. *Bloodlines: A Journey into Eastern Europe.* Vancouver: Douglas & McIntyre, 1993.

Kymlicka, Will. *Liberalism, Community, and Culture.* Oxford: Oxford University Press, 1991.

Kymlicka, Will. *Multicultural Citizenship: A Liberal Theory of Minority Rights.* Oxford: Oxford University Press, 1995.

Ladha, Mansoor. *A Portrait in Pluralism: The Aga Khan's Shia Ismaili Muslims.* Calgary: Detselig Enterprises, 2008.

Lam, Lawrence. *From Being Uprooted to Surviving: Resettlement of Vietnamese-Chinese "Boat People" in Montreal, 1980–1990.* Toronto: York Lanes Press, 1996.

McAllister, Kirsten Emiko. *Terrain of Memory: A Japanese Canadian Memorial Project.* Vancouver: UBC Press, 2010.

Nghia, Vo. *The Vietnamese Boat People, 1954 and 1975–1992.* Jefferson, NC: McFarland & Co., 2006.

Sajoo, Amyn B., ed. *A Companion to the Muslim World.* London, U.K.: I.B. Tauris, 2009.

Saul, John Ralston. *A Fair Country: Telling Truths About Canada.* Toronto: Penguin, 2008.

Suzuki, David T. *Metamorphosis: Stages in a Life.* Toronto: Stoddart, 1987.

Taylor, Charles. *The Malaise of Modernity.* Toronto: House of Anansi Press, 1991.

Taylor, Charles. *Multiculturalism: Examining the Politics of Recognition.* Princeton: Princeton University Press, 1994.

Wiebe, Rudy Henry. *Of This Earth: A Mennonite Boyhood in the Boreal Forest.* Toronto: Alfred A. Knopf Canada, 2006.

Woodcock, George, and Ivan Avakumovic. *The Doukhobors.* Toronto: McClelland & Stewart, 1977.

ACKNOWLEDGMENTS

Many people devoted time and energy to talk to me, and I am grateful to them for their help and enthusiasm.

Thanks to the mayor and people of Nelson, B.C.; J.J. Verigin and the Doukhobor community of Castlegar, B.C.; Damiano Pietropaolo and Ken Greenberg; and Merritt and Arlene Long, who shared their moving sponsorship story with me.

Thanks to David Davidar, who first suggested the idea for this book.

Support was constant from Gillian Hewitt Smith and everyone at the Institute for Canadian Citizenship.

Thanks to Michael Levine as always. And for their help, Diane Turbide, Sandra Tooze, Mary Opper, and Yvonne Hunter at Penguin Canada. Special kudos to Alex Schultz for his meticulous attention to detail. Thanks to Michael Henry, technology and research expert, and thanks to Micheline Steals.

As always, my appreciation to John Ralston Saul for his fine perceptions and his rapid recovery from his dismay thirty-five years ago that I did not speak Chinese.

INDEX